About tl

Born in 1933, Eleanor Milner was brought up on an East Yorkshire farm during wartime. She decided at an early age that she wanted to become a nurse and trained at Hull Royal Infirmary, before qualifying as a midwife at Liverpool Maternity Hospital. Returning to her native East Yorkshire, she accepted a post as a district nurse/midwife. She married in 1958 and moved to the Lincolnshire coast where her husband was the village sub-postmaster, and in 1964, the couple adopted a handicapped baby girl.

Eleanor returned to district nursing, later specialising in the care of the elderly, but a serious road accident in 1983 necessitated her premature retirement. Following her husband's untimely death, she took over the running of the village shop and was appointed sub-postmistress, later retiring to a bungalow in the village. She now lives near her daughter in Derbyshire, where she continues to enjoy her retirement.

The title, *98.4°F to 37°C*, being the decimal change in the measuring of normal body temperature, has been chosen to reflect the changes in nursing and social history over the last seventy years.

98.4° F TO 37° C
THE MEMOIRS OF
ELEANOR MILNER SRN SCM DNC

ELEANOR MILNER

98.4° F TO 37° C
THE MEMOIRS OF ELEANOR MILNER
SRN SCM DNC

With Regards

Eleanor Milner

Vanguard Press

A CIP catalogue record for this title is
available from the British Library.

ISBN 978 1 80016 258 7

*Vanguard Press is an imprint of
Pegasus Elliot MacKenzie Publishers Ltd.*
www.pegasuspublishers.com

First Published in 2021

**Vanguard Press
Sheraton House Castle Park
Cambridge England**

Printed & Bound in Great Britain

Dedication

My grateful thanks go to my daughter, Mary, who encouraged me when I faltered, for our shared tears and laughter, and for her patience and secretarial skills throughout the writing of this book.

I would also like to thank my nursing colleagues, my patients and their relatives, and not forgetting our village customers and friends.

Contents

Prologue

After enjoying small dinner parties with our friends who had lived different lifestyles and pursued varying career paths, we would lazily sit back with a glass or two and reminisce. An 'off the cuff' remark would set one or another off to tell a tale. "Write it down," a friend persisted but I prevaricated until one evening sitting in the gloaming with 'nothing decent' on the television, I let my thoughts wander and started to write. I could not stop – it was difficult to know what to leave out.

I have chosen the title of *98.4⁰F to 37⁰C '*, this being the decimal change in the measuring of normal blood temperature and thus reflecting changes in nursing and social history over the last seventy years.

My grateful thanks must go to my daughter, Mary, who encouraged me when I faltered, for our shared tears and laughter, and for her patience and secretarial skills throughout the writing of this book.

Chapter 1 – Early Years

I had a happy childhood growing up on a farm in the East Riding of Yorkshire, not fully understanding the perils and dangers of wartime particularly as we lived not far from the Humber Estuary. Hull was one of the most bombed cities outside London.

My earliest recollection was regaining consciousness, having fallen from one of my father's shire horses. Her name was 'Patch', a grey mare. She was fat and perhaps pregnant at the time, and her back was very shiny and slippery. We had the birth of a foal nearly each year, allowing the mother to rest whilst the other horses continued to work the land. I had been carried into the large living kitchen and placed on a chaise longue which was oozing horsehair and I can remember the hair prickling my legs. Fortunately, the only thing damaged was my pride!

War was declared three months before my twin brother and sister were born. This must have been scary for my mother having already had me and my younger sister. My first memory of the twins was their christening at the parish church. It was winter and a bitterly cold day. My task during the ceremony was to hold the vicar's glasses. I can also remember crying and hating the doctor who was immunising the twins against diphtheria, polio and whooping cough. Two of our cousins had contracted polio, resulting in permanent disability. One afternoon, Mum took us to Paull, a village on the River Humber about four miles away, to see the ships on the river, explaining why one of the ships was flying a yellow flag, indicating that a person on board was suffering from an infectious disease, and therefore, the ship was not allowed to dock in Hull.

Grandma lived at The Grange, a farm a few miles away. I never knew my grandfather as he had died when my own father was seven years old. He had contracted pneumonia whilst breaking in a horse. I have memories of visiting The Grange with my sister and joining Grandma and an auntie to make 'clippie' rugs. The base of the rug was hessian attached to a wooden frame, and we each had a peg which was used to attach clips of material to the hessian. These strips of material were cut from worn out clothes – recycling was very popular in those days, it had to be! The finished rugs protected our feet from the cold brick and concrete floors of the farmhouse.

Each year itinerant Irish workers would come over to England for the harvest (mainly white corn and potatoes) and from August through to November could often be found working on both my father's and grandmother's farms. Harvest time was much later in those days, often starting after the children had already returned to school for the autumn term. One particularly wet summer a field of beans (grown for cattle feed) was not brought into the stack yard until New Year's Day.

The itinerant workers on my grandmother's farm were always well fed. A trestle table would appear in the scullery and each man would be served a large Yorkshire pudding with gravy. The meat course would follow and then, as my uncle called it a 'stick to your ribs' pudding, i.e., jam roly-poly, spotted dick or fruit pie would finish off their meal. It was hardly surprising that the same workforce appeared each year.

I can also recall one particularly tuneful Irishman singing as he turned the churn over and over to make creamy home-made butter (in more recent years the butter churn has found a new use as a tombola machine!). During the war, two Irishmen returned as usual to help my father with the harvest, but this time only stayed one week. They were absolutely petrified about the bombs being dropped in Hull and surrounding area. Whether they went onto another farm further away from Hull and the bombs, or returned to Ireland, we never knew.

At the outbreak of war, the headmaster at the village primary joined our teacher, Miss Verity, and told us not to worry about the war as there were lots of soldiers protecting the King and Queen at Buckingham Palace. Gummed brown paper strips were stuck to the windows of the classroom, the idea being to stop the glass from shattering during explosions. Stories were read to us whilst we were sheltering in the school air raid shelter during daylight raids. I remember the tales of *Milly Molly Mandy* and *Brer Fox* and *Brer Rabbit*.

On exceptionally cold days, Miss Verity would put our wet gloves to dry in the mesh of the classroom fireguard. On the coal fire she would heat up a pan of milk to make cocoa for consumption during playtime, a welcome change from the third of a pint of cold milk in a glass bottle complete with cardboard lid and straw. I'm not sure how these activities would be rated by the risk assessor today!

During one night of heavy German air activity, we were in our air raid shelter with our mother. Father had dug the shelter in the garden, partially underground and built with straw bales covered in soil. The earth shook, and I can remember mother saying, "That's close." Dad was on fire watch. He came into the shelter saying that he had been blown off his feet by a number of bombs falling in our neighbour's field. It was later discovered that twelve bombs had exploded, leaving one unexploded. The Bomb Disposal Squad attended, disarming and loading the now harmless bomb onto the back of their lorry and showing us the results of their labours.

At school the following day I can remember going into the classroom when all of our desks had been moved around. We had to sit with a different classmate. I learned later that this was to try and hide the fact that two of our schoolmates had been killed during the overnight bombing. I also recall that we had to fold our arms and rest our heads on the desk for a half-hour's attempt at sleep.

Another frightening wartime memory was the dropping of numerous anti-personnel bombs which were known as butterfly bombs. Each bomb was the size of a two pound golden syrup tin fitted with a spindle with spinning vanes, which delayed the bomb's descent and staying silent on landing until someone unfortunately walked closely by, their vibration thus setting the bomb off. It was thought locally that the army camp next to our farm had been the intended target. During this attack two of our shire horses were sadly killed, and later on during harvest, the army came with a lightweight tank, and dragging the binder behind, cut the wheat for us (the twenty-one acre grass field where the horses had been killed had been dyked cross-ways in two places, to prevent enemy aircraft using the field as a landing site should an invasion occur).

A farm worker on a neighbouring farm had been taking a load of grain with two shire horses to the local corn merchants. He stepped off the main track to make room for the postman to go by and unfortunately set off a partially hidden butterfly bomb, killing him and mortally wounding the two horses which had to be shot. Nearly twenty years later, my father ploughed up another of these butterfly bombs which the army had missed at the time. The Bomb Disposal Squad was duly called once again and blew the offending item up, the only casualty this time being our lounge windows in the farmhouse.

My father was commissioned to clear brick rubble from a derelict site in the next village. This was useful material for building up gateways and filling ruts in the farm tracks. My sister and I had taken the opportunity of having a ride on the cart, and after loading the rubble, we were parked in the market place, as we waited for Dad to come out of the bank. A youth carrying an antique car horn chose to blow it just as he walked by the horses. They then panicked and took off down the main road. A man walking by, who only had one arm, saw the unfolding danger and somehow managed to climb up onto the back of the cart. He grabbed the reins, finally pulling all of us safely to a halt just before the crossroads. Being ever grateful, my father went back into the bank to reward our rescuer. He also had the rather difficult job of explaining the incident to my mother!

We had a paraffin heated incubator for hatching chicks, and I can remember my sister and I being supervised as we helped to turn the eggs. We would splash a little water on each egg, which would then be turned, just as a mother hen would do when settling on the nest. Towards the end of the three-week hatching period, we were allowed to pick up each egg to listen for any cheeping.

We also used paraffin to light the lamps in the farmhouse from which I was able to see to do my homework. Calor gas, which was much more convenient and gave us brighter light, did not arrive until after the war had ended. A copper in the corner of the scullery was used for doing the laundry. The grate would be made ready for Dad to light in the early morning before going out to milk the cows. The water in the copper would then be hot enough for Mum to use after we had gone to school. This system for the laundry remained in place until 1954 when electricity was finally installed on the farm.

The family had been supplied with gas masks. I had a black mask, smaller but similar to my parents'. Being slightly younger, my sister had a Mickey Mouse red one and the twins had their own canvas cots, each fitted with a pump action valve. On rainy days taking our masks to school, the cardboard boxes would get wet and so, to preserve the masks, Mum bought us special mask tins with shoulder straps in which to carry them.

Towards the end of the war, ten Italian prisoners from a local camp were sent to help my dad with the farm work. They objected to the 'farm smells' and wanted to eat their lunch in the farmhouse rather than in the warm cow shed. My father said, "They're useless, all they do is stand and comb their hair!" Eventually he lost his patience and they were never sent to us again. Later, from the same POW camp came two German prisoners. Gerhardt had left school to join the German army but was captured within six weeks. Josef, who was much older, was not physically strong and had not been recruited very long before he too was captured. They were both much more willing to learn and were a good help on the farm, Dad and Gerhardt would take on the heavier tasks, leaving the lighter work to Josef. To prevent prisoners escaping a piece of material would be removed from the back of their jacket and replaced by a patch of a very different colour. Both Gerhardt and Josef kept in touch with us after they had been repatriated, but their correspondence eventually faded.

VE Day arrived, but this was much like any other day for me. My sister and I were allowed to go down to the village, but had to return home before the celebrations had really got started.

A final memory regarding 'clippie' rugs – we had two large ones in the scullery which were very heavy and would have to be dragged into the garden to be beaten with a twisted willow carpet beater. Dad had bought a two-stroke petrol mower which was very temperamental. Tinkering with it in the warmth of the scullery, he pulled the starter cable. The mower shot off leaving a bare pathway and clips flying all around. I can remember the look of horror on his face! My mother was secretly rather pleased about this, as she could now finally dispose of them and replace them with the more fashionable coconut matting. The damaged 'clippie' rugs found a new home in the dog kennel!

Following primary school I started at Withernsea Secondary Modern School. However, apparently, I had decided that I wanted to be a nurse at quite a young age, and so, to help me fulfil my dream, my mother made enquiries about the most appropriate school to give me a head start. With the assistance of my present headmaster, and my mother combined, I obtained a place at Estcourt High School for Girls in Hull, where pre-nursing and commerce courses were held.

During my second year at Estcourt High School I was recruited by our biology teacher to join the Red Cross where we, as cadets, learnt to make splints from wood and cotton wool. We were also told how to roll bandages and make other basic first aid dressings – a capelin bandage was the ultimate test for bandaging a scalp. This involved two bandages being used at the same time, one going round the forehead and the other backwards and forwards over the top of the scalp. On removal the test was that it had to stay in one piece looking rather like a helmet.

During the Festival of Britain in 1951, HMS Campania, a floating exhibition hall, sailed into Hull, and as part of my Red Cross duties, I did an afternoon shift on board. The only casualty was a stewardess who somehow managed to crack her head on a staircase. Fortunately, a ship's officer came to the rescue and I stood down.

Having passed the relevant examinations, I moved to Hull Technical College for a year's course on Applied Human Biology, trying to remember the names of different glands, nerves and blood groups etc. This led onto an interview with Matron at the old Hull Royal Infirmary. This building was replaced by a new hospital in 1967, a familiar landmark in the city today.

Chapter 2 – Nurse Training

"You will live in – no option! You will need to bring in your National Identity Card and ration book, and also a washable named laundry bag." Butter, sugar, bacon and some other food stuff, were still rationed in 1951. Also, the instruction, "Go to your doctor to be immunised against typhoid, polio and diphtheria."

The nurses' home was a dull place, bottle green paint below the dado line and a mustard cream above, with unlit corridors. The wooden floors, however, shone. The girls were a jolly lot, with many a prank played. In the schoolroom of PTS (Preliminary Training School) were two single hospital beds and one cot. A male dummy occupied one bed, a female the other, and a sexless baby in the cot. One weekend when Sister Tutor was away, a prankster placed the two adult dummies in one bed, with the cot close by. Unfortunately, PTS was overlooked by some flats, and a concerned resident telephoned the hospital convinced that the 'patients' were being neglected and at least one person was dead! To convince her that all was well, she was invited to see for herself!

Thinking about pranksters reminds me of one particular Christmas. Situated outside the front door of the hospital (only used by Matron and the hospital secretary) stood a white marble statue of one of the founding fathers', who during the night adorned himself in red crepe paper. Unfortunately, it rained during the early hours and the next day a porter was dispatched to disrobe him of his now soggy pink outfit. I think that the old chap enjoyed the situation as he wore a rather rosy glow for several weeks!

We all gained weight as Sister Tutor fed us toast and jam, and milky coffee. "Don't worry, you'll soon run it off once you are on the wards." How right she was! The food itself, however, was awful. This was my introduction to tripe and onions, kippers, and rabbit stew. I seemed to get the rabbit's ribcage each time, and I have never eaten rabbit since!

During PTS we were shown how to fold our starched caps. Initially these were very similar to mop caps, but as our training progressed, more folds were introduced into the making of these caps until they eventually perched onto the top of our heads. White hairgrips were a necessity to keep this stylish headgear in place. Chevrons, either two or three stripes, also had to be stitched onto our uniform sleeve to denote our seniority. I can remember being accosted in the corridor by the assistant matron, "Where are your chevrons, nurse?" I hadn't had time to find a needle and cotton!

"Volunteers, you," – Yes, me – "Get into this iron lung," came the barked command from our tutor. This iron lung was a coffin-like enclosed box with my head poking out the end, with a rubber flange around my neck. I initially wasn't too keen on this new experience but once I was able to relax and allow the machine to breath for me, I wasn't nearly so panicky. However, I realised this must have been a truly awful experience for the patients entombed in this machine twenty-four hours a day. Poliomyelitis was the usual cause of paralysis of the chest wall.

It was during the early days of PTS that we had to watch (from a distance) an operation in theatre. Sister Tutor and Theatre Sister would select a candidate choosing the appropriate operation to be attended. We stood close to the wall, sister tutor whispering occasionally. I think it was to keep our concentration. On reflection, I suspect this was to sort out the would-be fainters from the more stoic – fortunately I fell into the latter group. The usual operation was an appendicectomy, but I learned later that I had been present during an operation on a pilonidal sinus (this occurs as the result of an in-growing hair in the cleft at the top of the buttocks which can cause severe pain and become infected). I only ever nursed two patients suffering from this condition.

Our working week comprised of forty-five hours (frequently more voluntarily). The day started at seven twenty a.m. and ended at seven thirty p.m. with a three-hour break either ten thirty to one thirty, two to five p.m., or finishing at five p.m. We had one and a half days off a week; sometimes the half day consisted of a 'long morning' when we didn't start work until one thirty p.m. We had four weeks annual leave broken into three separate breaks, though the foreign nurses (mainly Irish) were allowed to take their holiday in one block. Naturally we worked every bank holiday unless our normal day off fell at this time.

We started the day wearing yesterday's apron and after bedpan rounds and other 'dirty' care, we would dash to our rooms to change into a new stiffly starched apron and then we went for our coffee break. There was very little privacy for patients on the ward. Screens with squeaky wheels were put in front of the ward doorway, announcing that the bedpan round was taking place. During treatment rounds, however, individual screens were put around the beds. Pressure areas were treated with surgical spirit. Our hands were scrubbed with Dettol and dried on the dressing towel, which had previously been autoclaved. On finishing the dressing round, we were offered some hand cream which was kept in sister's office. However, no one was ever allowed to be over-enthusiastic with it!

Having finished PTS training, I was allocated to a Female Surgical Ward. Sister was very protective of the junior girls; only more senior nurses cared for the dying. Senior members of the Red Cross would often do voluntary work on the wards, and to relieve the nurses for other duties, would sometimes sit with the dying. Sister asked me to take a cup of tea to the Red Cross lady. On moving a screen, I found myself face to face with my old biology teacher. She was pleased to see that I had followed my dream.

For those going into hospital today, how things have changed. I can remember prepping patients prior to their surgery, who were dressed in white gowns, knee socks made from abb wool (really trawler men's socks) and triangular scarves to cover ladies' heads. After their pre-med injection and once the patient had been taken to theatre, a cage containing electric bulbs was placed on the bed so that there was a warm return. Post-operative recovery took place on the ward, so post-op bowls containing tongue forceps and a vomit bowl was placed on the locker in readiness for the patient's return from theatre. The ward I was working on had two oxygen cylinders, but only one mask. The second one had disappeared, but in a real emergency we borrowed one from the ward above. This was on a twenty-six bedded ward, with frequently three extra beds added down the middle of the ward.

On completion of our first year, we finally managed to acquire nylon stockings. The thick grey lisle we had previously worn, which were torpedo-proof but at least did not ladder, were gladly discarded. We had had to darn the toes and heels whenever a hole appeared. The suspenders conducted electricity, and we got many a shock from the metal bedsteads. Aided by the red rubber mackintoshes, some patients seemed to produce more static!

Hull Royal Infirmary had a sister hospital, Sutton Annexe, which was in the countryside on the outskirts of Hull. Here were Male Surgery, Female Surgery, Male and Female Medical wards, and a Children's Ward, each with a balcony. Patients suffering from TB were placed outside on the balcony, even during a snowstorm, only retreating to the day room when thick fog was prevalent. It was at this time we had a Mantoux test followed by BCG vaccination.

In the mid-1950s a request from the government had gone out to the colonies for plumbers, carpenters and nurses to help put the country back on its feet after the loss of life and devastation from the war years. Mentioning our salary situation to Sister, she replied, "You are lucky to be getting paid during your training; my parents had to pay for me to train." To my youthful enthusiasm she seemed as old as Methuselah, but she was a very good teacher.

The recruitment of nurses willing to train in the big city hospitals was particularly difficult, as industry competed for the available workforce with wages which, in our eyes, were comparatively generous. To further illustrate this problem, two of my compatriots who had been through nurse training courses at school, technical college and PTS, then left their nurse training due to a mixture of antisocial hours and the poor pay. I also believe that their parents had needed the increased financial help to raise their younger siblings. My younger sister, aged seventeen, was a shorthand typist for a local shipping firm. Her salary was thirty-three per cent more than mine, when I was a qualified nurse aged twenty-one.

The buzz in the nurses' sitting room was about a promised pay rise. Our pay packets revealed that this was not absolutely true. Income tax and emoluments (nurses' home bed and board) had taken the extra cash and we were actually worse off in our pockets than before the rise. This was eventually rectified twelve weeks later.

A fourteen-year-old boy was admitted to Male Surgical (it was debated whether he should have been taken to the children's hospital in Park Street). He was suffering multiple injuries. A lorry driver had opened his cab door, knocking the boy into the path of an oncoming lorry. On being prepared to go to theatre for a second time, a foreign national suffering horrific burns from the explosion of a ship's boiler got out of bed, and on his knees, prayed for the lad. There was many a glisten in both patients and nurses' eyes. The chap didn't like hospital food (well, who did!) and our male charge nurse would curry eggs for him as a supplement. The boy was an inpatient for many weeks and I had been moved to another ward before his discharge.

A rather tall man appeared in the ward corridor. "Hello nurse, I've come to see Mr Stevens." This was out of visiting hours and I explained that the doctor was with the patient. I sat him down amongst the potted palms in the day room.

"Good morning, sir," was the greeting of the houseman as he emerged from the ward door. I dashed to the linen room to hide my embarrassment; I had mistaken him for a solicitor. Members of the legal profession were allowed to visit the ward out of visiting hours.

Elective surgery was the order of the day, where operations were scheduled and the level of post-operative care could be planned. I was now coming to the end of my second year. I had escorted many patients to theatre, though only staying as 'dogsbody' to do any required task until the time came to accompany my patient back to the ward – I had never actually 'scrubbed'. And so, it was now my turn to work in theatre and I had to learn the names and usage of the various surgical instruments. Theatre work is not as glamorous as it sounds, as my first instruction was to wash the floor between operations with hot soapy water and a squeezy mop. I then graduated to 'scrubbing up' to assist at the operating table. I can recall one gall bladder operation when I had to use some very large retractors to keep the wound open on a particularly obese patient.

After a few weeks I was given the responsibility to act as 'sister'. This is a nominal title which involved handing the relevant instruments to the surgeon. The actual theatre sister would stand supervising from a distance but was available to assist if needed. Much to my alarm, the surgeon operating that day was the same surgeon who I had put among the potted palms. However, he was the most patient and tolerant of men and was extremely popular with the nurses and house surgeons alike; he had either forgotten or was too polite to mention my earlier faux pas. Theatre work was not my favourite part of training as the patients came in unconscious and returned to the ward in the same state.

There were no operations on the day of the coronation of Queen Elizabeth II, but this was no day off for us and considered to be an ideal opportunity to catch up on theatre housekeeping. While many in the country watched proceedings taking place in the capital, glued to their (or their neighbour's) newly acquired television set, we were busy packing dressing drums, sterilising instruments and patching rubber gloves. A type of bicycle puncture kit was supplied for this task.

The surgeons, of course, preferred not to use the patched gloves, but the registrars and house surgeons did accept them, but only with no more than two patches per glove. 'Scrubbed' nurses had to wear what was available after that, no matter what the size. I have small hands and take size six, if size seven and a half had to be used the finger ends were full of talcum powder, therefore, making it difficult to thread the needles.

One night, I was on night duty alone, on a twenty-bedded ward but with a runner (a junior nurse who during busy periods shared her time with mine and another ward). At two a.m. I was busily occupied recording temperatures and blood pressures, when an elderly man suddenly burst his stitches. On lifting the bedclothes, I was horrified at the awful sight of his intestines and rapidly covered the open wound with sterile towels. The patient concerned had undergone surgery some seven days earlier when a dermoid cyst containing teeth and bones and weighing over ten pounds had been removed. Quickly calling Night Sister who in turn called the duty surgical houseman, the old gentleman was rushed back to theatre, with Night Sister acting as the theatre sister. He was re-stitched and returned to the ward, wearing a 'many-tailed' bandage. Sadly, two anaesthetics within seven days proved too much for his constitution, and he peacefully passed away a few days later.

'Many-tailed' bandages consisted of a padded square of flannelette with eighteen-inch tails coming from the sides of the square. According to the patients with pendulous abdomens, these bandages were very comforting, the interleaving of the tails proving very supportive. During slacker periods on the ward, usually during visiting time, we nurses were kept busy stitching these 'many tails' and also packing dressings into drums prior to autoclaving.

Due to the extra workload during that night, the disturbance had woken several patients asking for drinks and urinals. I was late taking the six a.m. temperatures and blood pressures when I realised that I was one thermometer short. To my relief, I found it still where it had been placed in the old gentleman's armpit!

Any losses or breakages had to be paid for by depositing one shilling into Matron's office. The thermometers were kept in a meat paste jar with cotton wool in the base soaked in Dettol. The dangers of mercury are now well known and should not come into contact with skin and most certainly not swallowed! Thankfully we now use digital thermometers.

Another night on a quiet ward, I heard a rustling, surely not a mouse! On investigating further, I discovered a diabetic patient helping himself to mince pies previously brought in by his wife. It was hardly surprising that we could not get his sugar levels balanced, and my interrogation certainly answered a few questions.

A lot of male patients (and some female), particularly after surgery, suffered from a productive cough, I suspect from heavy smoking which was very common during the fifties, and was even allowed on the wards. The sparks from one old gentleman's pipe actually left burn holes in the linen. Lysol or Dettol was placed in the bottom of the sputum mugs, which were kept on the top of the locker, with care being taken only to put water into the mugs supplied to the confused, for obvious reasons.

One of our daily jobs was to note the quantity of the expectorant and then to clean the mugs by pressure washing in the sluice, occasionally the pressure working before or after the cleaning process. Later, when working as a nurse on the district, very often a blue and white striped coffee mug would be brought into use for this purpose. I have since then always refused refreshment produced in that popular Cornishware.

On one occasion when I had been invited to go to a local dance, I approached Home Sister for a late pass (she was unofficial guardian of we student nurses as we were still under twenty-one). "Why don't you get in, like you did last week?" she asked with a twinkle in her eye! At least she didn't ask for my escort's name and occupation, as Assistant Matron had previously done during Home Sister's leave. The previous week I had arrived back late from visiting my parents, and after taking off my precious nylons, I climbed the coke heap (which was conveniently outside the downstairs loo) and scrambled in through the unlocked window, praying that the last person had flushed!

My paternal grandmother (living at The Grange) made winceyette nightgowns for use on the Children's Ward in the newly built Sutton Annexe (built in 1933). She used either pink or blue embroidery silks to smock the yokes (smocking is a term used for embroidery stitches holding the little pleats together). Working on the Children's Ward I recognised her beautiful handiwork on the only surviving gown left in the linen cupboard, but at least this had survived nineteen years of hospital laundering.

I spent Christmas Eve night on the Children's Ward. One little girl, Mandy, could not sleep. Her parents had told her about Father Christmas. She was still awake at one a.m., and in desperation I carried her around the other wards. On the end of every bed there was an abb wool sock containing toiletries, a gift from the Patients' Fund. Surprise! Father Christmas had already visited on our return to the Children's Ward. This was an eye opener for me seeing the reactions of the other children. I remember that one little boy forgot his new toy and played with the box and brown paper and string, a scenario which must be familiar to many parents. Some parcels had been left by parents, but most had been supplied by the hospital, again from the Patients' Fund.

During a visit from Matron, Mandy had somehow acquired a boiled sweet and got it stuck in her throat. I grabbed her, and turning her upside down, with a heavy hand hit her between her shoulder blades – out came the sweetie across the floor, but in a split second she escaped my grasp, grabbed the sweet and it was back in her mouth. Matron raised her eyebrows, said nothing and continued on her rounds.

Our bedding in the nurses' home at Sutton Annexe consisted of 'donkey breakfast' mattresses which were made of flock, which were periodically upgraded from redundant ones from the wards. The central heating never seemed to be working properly and we all used our red-lined capes in addition on top of the bed. The khaki and grey blankets provided by the hospital were totally inadequate for their purpose, but it was my mother (the ever-practical one) who had bought me a fluffy white blanket for my birthday, this being in the middle of June!

A paper boy would do a 'round' on the hospital wards selling daily morning papers. He did good business as did the WVS trolley – I think their most popular lines were biscuits and Palmolive soap. I had a keen sense of smell and would get a whiff on opening the patient's locker. I would comment when there was a change to a different product, usually Imperial Leather. The hospital library trolley was another service run by these volunteers. The WVS (Women's Voluntary Service) was awarded its Royal status in 1966 by Queen Elizabeth II becoming the WRVS. In 2013 this name was changed to the Royal Voluntary Service (RVS), an organisation that continues its good work today.

On the Women's Ward one could often detect lavender water or 4711 eau de cologne, with its distinctive bottle and stopper proudly displayed on the locker top. A colleague of mine's mother had peacefully died in the side ward. Sister asked me to attend and do the usual offices. In the middle of carrying out this procedure, Sister came in and generously sprinkled lavender water all over the bed and me. Before going for coffee, which was fortunately imminent, I dashed back to the nurses' home for a quick change of all my clothing.

Returning to Hull Royal Infirmary – by this time I was in my third year of training, and therefore, deemed responsible enough to be 'in charge' of a twenty-six bedded Nightingale ward, the term emanating from a well-known nurse from the Crimean War. Night Sister did three ward rounds between nine p.m. and six thirty a.m., the night report being delivered to her office by six a.m. One night whilst my junior who was busy (a second-year nurse), I did the medication round. An emergency admission was suffering from asthma. I left his Aminophylline suppositories (to relieve bronchial spasm) in a kidney dish on his locker, saying, "I will be back with the screens and a PR tray." On my return as promised, there in the dish were just the silver wrappers. "I'll get you a bowl of water to wash your hands," I offered.

"I would rather have a glass of water," he replied. "They took some swallowing."

I kept a special watch on him, as his blood pressure could have dropped suddenly as his blood vessels dilated (due to natural wastage, there is a greater concentration of a drug in its suppository form than in tablet form). The patient continued to prefer to administer his own treatment, but from then on, in the correct manner as prescribed!

Just two nights later, a call came from Casualty with the terse message, "Make up a 'shock' bed. The patient is going from here to theatre, then onto you." The bed near the ward sister's office usually held the most seriously ill so, after juggling bed number twenty-five to the middle of the ward, number twenty-six was moved down a place. A junior nurse and porter retrieved a spare bed from the stores. The stores was an unused ward, deemed not safe enough to be used as an active ward due to bomb damage received during air raids in the war.

All was ready with the electrically heated cage and the precarious wooden blocks to raise the bottom of the bed. After making our patient comfortable and now able to slow his blood transfusion, I wondered what on earth had happened to him. The night sister's reply was, "He has emasculated himself." He had somehow managed to travel in by bus from a village five miles away, resulting in a tremendous loss of blood. Emptying his pockets and washing his cash was not a very pleasant experience. He was carrying more money than my month's salary, about five pounds. I think he was visited by the psychiatrist whilst he was still on the ward. He was the first person that I knowingly met who was dissatisfied with his gender.

After sitting my SRN examination and while waiting for the results, short periods were spent on ears nose and throat (tonsillectomies and mastoidectomies being the main operations of the day), and then onto a spell on the Eye Ward. It was here that I learned to do sub-conjunctival injections, administering the drug directly into the eye. At the time this was a daily procedure carried out by nurses, who were considered to have the more dexterous fingers, a procedure now more likely to be left to the doctors.

During a night duty on ENT, a rather well-dressed gentleman walked onto the ward. Remembering my earlier faux pas, I asked him who he was. He identified himself as one of the ENT surgeons. "I am asking a favour, will you syringe my ears, please?"

I was taken aback at his request and replied, "I have not been trained to syringe ears."

"Don't worry, I will guide you." He nipped to the Male Surgical Ward and borrowed a bladder syringe, while I got towels, a receiver and a jug of warm water. The procedure was a success. To my surprise, he returned the bladder syringe, and with a quiet word of thanks, he went on his way. A few weeks later when I was working on Casualty, he spotted me and said, "You have cost me a new car – I heard all the squeaks and knocks on my old one!"

Many years later when I was recounting this story to an old friend and colleague, who was visiting from Australia, she asked me whether he was carrying a furled umbrella. "I don't think so," I replied. "Why?" She recounted her own story of 'someone' putting a handful of cornflakes in the umbrella!

During this same visit she mentioned that her mother had been disappointed with the care her husband (my friend's father) had received during his last hours at the hospital. I was able to reassure her that all that was possible had been done for him. The casualty officer had run alongside the stretcher as he had been admitted to the ward. He had straddled the patient while still on the stretcher carrying out external heart massage (now CPR), sadly to no avail. Her father had then been laid on a bed to allow the nurses to carry out the last offices. My friend had been unaware of my presence at the time.

During our Casualty training we were taught to stitch wounds. Our first efforts would be on scalps, the resulting scars would not be seen, we hoped, for many a year. We could smell the casualties from the St Andrew's Fish Dock before they even arrived. I remember one chap who had virtually filleted his arm. The artery and vein could be seen either side of the wound. "I'll give the locals," said the doctor. "You stitch, you'll be a better needlewoman than me." I am pleased to say that the smell emanating from his overalls did not put me off eating fish dinners.

If any patient was unaccompanied on admission, their outdoor clothes would be stored in the clothes cupboard to be collected on discharge. What a shock – the first time I opened the cupboard door an artificial leg, complete with brown lace-up shoe, hit me on the head. Apparently, this had lived there for several months, the history of its owner long forgotten but now a source of amusement to the staff who had previously fallen foul of its presence.

On the Female Eye Ward, we had prayers at eight a.m. We were not obliged to attend, but did get the 'eye' from Sister if we were absent. There was no suitable space for prayers on the Male Ward as this was circular with a very large central pillar.

It was during this time I also undertook the role of acting staff nurse on Casualty. However, if a successful candidate applied for a nursing post and then subsequently passed their examinations, it was very likely that they would be offered the post on a permanent basis. Of course, we were only paid student rates until we received our SRN results. Often nurses, once qualified, moved on to do further nursing disciplines such as midwifery, ophthalmology (specialising in eyes) or children's nursing. Others left nursing altogether because they chose marriage, as was usual for those days. It would be a good, few years yet, before attitudes changed.

One day, a young woman walked into Casualty, heading straight for the staff toilets and sadly suffered a miscarriage. Realising that I hadn't a clue what to do, Sister took over from me to deal with this sad situation. Highlighting an obvious gap in my knowledge, it was there and then that I decided I wanted to do my midwifery training.

I had passed! A local dignitary presented us with our hospital badges, my SRN badge arriving by post. To celebrate the completion of my nurse training and becoming a State Registered Nurse, my mother bought me a silver buckle, so now I finally looked the part. I still treasure that silver buckle today.

Chapter 3 – Liverpool

I arrived in Liverpool with five other nurses, who had come from different parts of the UK, and was duly met at the midwives' home by Sister Tutor. This would be our home for the next six months. It was an opulent-looking house situated in Abercrombie Square which was within walking distance of the maternity hospital. There was a convenient bus route for either going into town or out to Hunts Cross where my aunt lived. It was from Abercrombie Square where I started my driving lessons. I clearly remember driving round Prince's Park on 'kangaroo' petrol.

Although it was a Sunday we were set to work immediately. "Ladies you may be surprised by the fact that we do not deliver babies at this maternity hospital. WE DELIVER MOTHERS. A woman is delivered of her offspring and you will see that babies do not arrive in cardboard boxes. Remember in the Bible, mother Mary was delivered of a son and any announcement of a Royal Birth states that the Queen or a Princess was delivered of…"

We were each allocated to a ward. I was sent to an Antenatal Ward. A helpful fellow trainee told me that, on hearing the labour bell (which told us that a birth was imminent), with Sister's permission, to get gowned and masked and make a dash to witness the birth. Labour Ward had gleaming white tiles and screens (again with squeaky wheels), a crowd gathered around the bottom of the bed with doctors and other pupil midwives witnessing the delivery. I was at the back of the crowd but didn't go unnoticed. My eyes must have been popping. "Are you all right, nurse?" Sister asked.

"Yes, thank you, but isn't it a peculiar colour?" There were ripples of laughter.

"Thank God it is," came her reply! The baby boy was a wonderful shade of purple. "When did you start here?" Sister enquired.

"This morning," I answered.

"You shouldn't be here, but since you are, I'll sign your witness book." A pupil midwife had to witness ten births before being allowed to work on the Labour Ward. However, I was the proud owner of having an entry in my book, having witnessed a delivery on my very first day.

I think that it was about my third or fourth witnessed delivery when a woman walked into the Maternity Hospital in labour. There was no antenatal history on file and neither had she booked with a midwife elsewhere. Quickly the Labour Ward Sister, taking immediate control, decided that she would be the 'catcher' and the staff midwife would be in charge of the mother. A baby boy arrived issuing a high-pitched scream rather than the usual cry. The delivering midwife explained, "He's for cold turkey, I'm afraid." This baby was already addicted to drugs, as was his mother. He was taken away to be slowly 'dried out'. I never heard what happened to either mother or baby, and thankfully this was the only delivery of this kind that I have ever witnessed. On another occasion one mother arrived at the hospital in a distressed state and gave birth to triplets. She also had not sought any antenatal care or booked with a midwife. Fortunately, her two boys and a girl arrived safely, but these triplets only counted as one delivery in my book.

The emergency bell rang and Sister said, "Join me in setting up theatre for a Caesarean section." The bell rang again. "You did theatre training during your nurse training?"

"Yes," I replied.

"Organise someone to catch the baby, you, 'scrub'." On these instructions, she quickly left to assist with a particularly difficult delivery on the Labour Ward. Feeling rather thrown in at the deep end, I hurried to theatre and scrubbed as ordered. The surgeon on call arrived and carried out a 'horseshoe' Caesarean section, happily delivering the mother safely of her baby. I think the more common technique used today is what is known as the 'bikini line' whereas previously a vertical incision had been the surgical preference.

The crash team was an important part of the hospital midwifery team and the members on call for this team varied according to the duty rota. As I was nearing the end of my training in Liverpool, during one shift I was suddenly given the command to, "Pick up the bags, and follow me." I was actually on duty on postnatal ward, but as I was nearing the end of my training, was also on duty with a staff midwife for crash visits. It was felt that one could be spared from a lying in ward. The equipment we would need was already assembled in readiness for an urgent call.

The registrar, a medical student, staff nurse and I quickly arrived at our patient's address, having been ferried by ambulance with its bells ringing – I can remember feeling absolutely nauseous. I wasn't sure whether this was from sheer fright and fear of what we would find, or from our rather hasty and uncomfortable ambulance journey. The mother was delivered by forceps but her baby was very poorly. The attending district midwife was shocked quietly watching the unfolding scene. She silently helped me to pick up all the equipment and I cleaned the delivery bedroom as best I could. We then all got back into the ambulance with mum and baby for the return trip to the maternity hospital. I had a rather sleepless night going over and over this event in my mind. Thankfully the baby survived, with mother and baby staying in the maternity hospital for seven days before being transferred to a convalescent home at Southport. This was the only crash team visit I was ever called to attend.

What to do next! Matron sent for me. "Oh, I must have failed!" I thought and so with trepidation I knocked on her door.

She was smiling, "Sit down, what are your future plans?" I had never dared to contemplate the future – dealing with the present was enough for me. She continued, "I always keep three places on the district training course for my top three pupils, are you interested?" CMB (Certified Midwifery Board) Part one allowed a maternity nurse to attend a mother in labour, providing that a doctor or qualified midwife was in attendance. To actually be in charge of a delivery, you needed Part two of the CMB qualification. As I was free, I immediately took her up on her offer and our conversation concluded. "Go home for a week and report back here on Monday."

I had chosen to do my midwifery training in Liverpool to be near my aging aunt who had previously suffered a stroke. She had been very kind to us as children, and together with my sister, we had often spent happy holidays with her and my uncle. My mother used to place both of us into the care of the guard on the train from Hull to Liverpool and on approaching the Woodhead tunnel we always had to remember to close the railway carriage window to prevent us choking from the dense smoke emitting from the coal fired engine.

It was during my time in Liverpool that I learnt my housecraft, as my mother had been in the fortunate position to employ a cleaning lady. My aunt was very pleased that I would now be staying on in the city, and I was able to continue helping her with shopping and cleaning on my days off. It was during this second part of my midwifery training that she suffered another stroke which thankfully she survived. A good many years later she passed away in Hull Royal Infirmary succumbing to a third stroke whilst on holiday on my parent's farm.

The nurses' home was situated in a row of large Victorian terraced houses which were on a tram route. The houses were slightly set back from the pavement with an 'areaway', a small sunken area allowing light into the basement rooms. The coal store was located under the pavement, the coal man lifting a metal plate in the pavement to deliver his usual two bags of coal. The kitchen and scullery were situated in the basement from where we could see the legs of people passing by. The ground floor had a large sitting room at the front and a dining room at the back. On the first floor was Sister's and staff midwife's bedrooms and a bathroom used by all. We pupil midwives had our own rooms on the top floor. Demolition of some of the slums in the area had already taken place. You could still see the evidence of the foundations of the old houses and narrow streets, leaving the Church of St Francis Xavier standing alone.

Dorothy was the senior pupil, and her parents lived about thirty miles away. One day she telephoned the nurses' home to say that she would be late back from her day off due to the train drivers' walkout and strike – unfortunately a common occurrence at that time. A call for the midwife came in. "You go, just keep the kettle boiling until Dorothy and I get to you."

On arrival at the address the mother was well on with her labour, but there was neither a bed nor table in the room, only a mattress on the floor. After spreading out newspaper (a very precious commodity) on the floor, I laid out all my equipment, and on my knees, I attended her. All too soon her baby arrived, thankfully uneventfully. After completing the care, I was busy packing up my bowls and receivers when Sister and Dorothy walked in. "You shouldn't have done that," was the comment from Sister.

My rather shocked reply came, "Well, I can't put it back."

"She certainly cannot," was the quick response from the mother! That was my first unaccompanied delivery, the first of many.

At the time of my training, during the 'lying in' period a mother and baby were visited twice daily for three days, and then daily for a further eleven days. We carefully recorded temperatures, bathed the baby and took general care of the mother. The timing of our visits gradually got later in the day, as precedence was given to our new mums during the morning. Sister accompanied me on several of these visits, and on one occasion I was extremely glad that she was with me.

We found the baby very cold and floppy. Sister immediately leapt into action opening her dress and pressing the baby to her bare bosom. "Get the ambulance, there's a phone box at the end of the street," she ordered (not many of our patients had a telephone in those days). The ambulance duly arrived and quickly transported Sister, mother and baby to the hospital. After putting Sister's bike into the front room and locking up the house remembering to put the key on its string back through the letterbox, I retrieved my own bike and carried on with my visits. Mum and baby arrived safely back home three weeks later.

We usually disposed of the placenta (afterbirth) by wrapping it in newspaper and burning it on the open fire. A few houses had gas fires as their source of heating and so we had to take the placenta back for disposal at the nurses' home on our coal fire. National dried milk tins proved very useful containers for this purpose. Being rather tired after a three a.m. callout, I was busy negotiating the tram crossing when I got the front wheel of my bike caught in the tram rail, spilling all the bags and my dried milk tin at the feet of the traffic controlling policeman. I was very relieved that the milk tin and its lid hadn't parted company! My kindly policeman stopped all the traffic and helped a rather red-faced, embarrassed, midwife right her bike, and to a cacophony of car horns, I was soon on my way again. "Next time, cross the tracks at right angles," was his advice.

To gain experience of examinations carried out throughout pregnancy we attended the antenatal clinics at a local GP surgery. "Wearing perfume, nurse?" was the question.

"No doctor," was my reply. "It's lavender water on my cuffs and hem, I'm told it deters lice, I picked one up here last week and I don't want another." I had originally picked up this tip from a female doctor at the maternity hospital.

One day, arriving back at the hospital from a local call, I had shot straight into the nearest cloakroom, stripping off to my bra and pants to search for an uninvited biting guest. The bar of wet soap was already in my hand searching for the demon in my uniform dress, when in dashed one of the obstetricians. "Having trouble, nurse?" she asked. I explained my predicament. "Give me the soap, there's one on your back." Slap went the soap. "Gosh it's a big one. It must have had a good feed!"

"Yes, on me!" With that, she shot into the toilet cubicle. Seeing her later, it was this doctor who had advised me to paint lavender water on the cuffs and hems of my dress to deter the little beasties, it certainly was not for flirting. Evening in Paris was a popular perfume at the time, and my preferred choice!

As by now I had gained more midwifery experience, I was moved back to the maternity hospital, and was occasionally attending home deliveries, without supervision, of women who lived in close proximity to the hospital. These were often very poor terraced houses, still with privies in the backyard though at least the toilets had been upgraded to flush ones. However, no one seemed to be responsible for their cleanliness, the stench was eye watering and there was no lighting.

During a night time waiting period at one of these houses, I desperately needed to spend a penny. I announced my needs, only to be offered a zinc bucket by the husband, who seemed prepared to stay in the room. "We never use the outside one during darkness. You never know who is hanging around, though the rats do usually disappear on hearing footsteps." I made a hasty decision to 'hang on', but come daylight, I was reluctantly forced to avail myself of the facilities. After that experience, I always made sure I 'had been' before going out on a call.

During the fifties most of us smoked cigarettes, and if we were attending a slow labour, we would readily accept a ciggy from an anxious husband and he would then accept one back from us. I was fortunate enough to have a rather good lighter, a trigger type, which had been a birthday present from a colleague. The labour was progressing well and the head just about to emerge, when we were suddenly plunged into darkness. We, namely the mum and I, called for help, but the husband had taken his anxieties to the pub! The lighter! Holding the precious illumination in my left hand and with great cooperation from mum, the precious offspring duly arrived. Neither mum nor I were singed! Thereafter I learned to keep a 'meter' shilling in my pocket for such an emergency.

It was still common practice in Liverpool for women to be 'churched'. This would involve the new mother attending the local, usually Roman Catholic, church to give thanks for a safe delivery. Many older ladies would not receive the new mum into their home unless this ceremony had taken place. Whether this was to encourage their faith, or just plain superstition, I never found out.

A very wealthy fellow pupil midwife owned a red sports car. Her family lived near Birkenhead and one afternoon when our off duties coincided, she asked, "Like a ride through the tunnel and get a decent meal at my parents?"

"Yes, please," was my quick response. Travelling in her open topped car, we received many admiring glances. Were they for us? I rather suspected that they were for the car, but we will never know!

If ever I had an evening off and the weather was fine, I would sometimes catch the ferry to New Brighton, enjoying a walk along the prom and returning on either the Daffodil or Iris, recalling those happy childhood holidays my sister and I had had with our aunt.

I passed my final examination and was now a Certified Midwife. There were plenty of vacancies for midwives in Liverpool, but I hankered after the fresh air of Yorkshire. Whenever I had been on leave and back at home on my parent's farm, I had always begged to be taken to Spurn Point, at the mouth of the Humber, to enable me to take in the fresh air and wide-open spaces.

Chapter 4 – District Nurse Midwife

I saw an advert in the *Nursing Mirror* for the position of nurse midwife in Bridlington, and the interview took place at the county offices in Beverley. I was asked to stay behind. One of my fellow applicants had come out and said that she had been offered the job. "Don't go yet," was the call from the Director of Nursing Services. "Would you be interested in another post in Anlaby, Willerby and Kirk Ella which has not yet been advertised?" This was a rather affluent area of Hull. I explained that I had not yet passed my driving test. I had been learning to drive in Liverpool but I had not sat the test. "Then we will give you six months to pass it," was her reply. "In the meantime, I'm sure your colleagues will take on the more distant calls." I was taken to see my new district and meet my colleagues. I would be one in a team of two district nurse midwives and one state registered nurse.

At that time these two roles were combined, and in some very rural counties, the post of health visitor was also incorporated in the job description. My more senior colleague, Nurse Danby (I never did find out her first name but she was known affectionately as 'Danny') was due to retire in three years. The other member of our team, Nurse Foley, was SRN trained only. Nurse Danby was a nurse and midwife but also had the extra qualification of being trained by the Queen's Imperial District Nursing Services (QIDNS). In 1887 the sum of around £70,000 had been raised by the general public to celebrate Queen Victoria's Golden Jubilee and thereby a national training service for district nurses was born. However, by the time of my district nurse training, the Local Health Authority had taken over this role.

I found lodgings in Willerby. The food was good, but the decor still pre-war. Everywhere hung photographs of my landlady's son in his army uniform. The ones in my bedroom (and there were several) slowly began to disappear after I had taken to turning his rather miserable face to the wall!

My first case was to attend an old lady to give her a 'chair bath'. When the ablutions were completed in front of a roaring Yorkshire range, I asked her for clean clothes. She pointed to two pairs of combinations on a suspended wooden airer which worked on a pulley system. "Which pair?"

"The ones with the bow windows," she replied. Getting hotter and hotter I struggled with the wretched garment. I then realised I had put them on her swollen leg and body sideways, but my excuse was that I had only previously met these garments in the casualty department when they had been frequently cut off to prevent further damage to already broken bodies. We had had the same problem with men's boiler suits incorporating Wellington boots.

Thinking about combinations, reminds me of an elderly lady in casualty who had unfortunately suffered a fractured neck of femur. Every item of clothing had been attached to the next layer with several safety pins. Knowing how expensive combinations were, I resisted the temptation to cut the clothing off and also rescued all the safety pins, and after washing them in Dettol, duly claimed them for the department. Brand new crepe bandages and the white open weave ones each contained their own safety pin. However, recycled ones from the hospital laundry did not, so my newfound crop of gold kept the casualty department supplied for several weeks.

My next visit on that first morning was to an elderly, rather confused lady suffering from short-term memory loss, but her long-term memory was also confusing everyone else as she had reverted back to the native Welsh of her childhood, a rarely heard and even less understood language in the East Riding of Yorkshire!

Each Wednesday afternoon I visited a holidaymaker who was staying with relatives on a rather remote farm. I had to cross two fields, opening and closing gates as I went, taking great care to avoid inquisitive cows and their droppings. On one particularly wet Wednesday afternoon as I was traversing one of the fields, I managed to pick up a puncture in my back tyre. Cursing my luck and moaning to the farmer's wife as she took my rain-soaked coat, she called her husband from the nearby barn. "I'll fix it," he said. Following instructions, I sat by the roaring Yorkshire range, my coat steaming on the fireguard. A lovely cup of frothy coffee was placed in my hand, which was a change from the usual 'camp' coffee. A gentle tap on my shoulder, "Nurse, your bike is ready." Embarrassed, I had fallen asleep. "You were ready for that nap, you brought our great nephew into the world last night, and I know what time you got back home." It was still raining, and my bike was loaded onto a tractor trailer, with me squashed into the cab with the farmer. I was taken all the way home, so good to remember such nice caring people.

I was taken under the wing of Nurse Danby. She had delivered almost a thousand mums. She had made a promise to herself that she would give a silver christening mug to her thousandth baby. Sadly, this milestone was not appreciated by its recipient. She later discovered that the silver gift had been pawned in favour of beer and betting!

One valuable piece of advice given to me during my midwifery training was to always keep my delivery book up to date, with the weeks of gestation, the sex and birth weight etc. I was thankful I had taken this advice, when a couple of years later I was called upon to give those details. Paternity was in doubt, the husband being in active army service at the time of conception. It was in the days before DNA testing and I still wonder whether his doubts were ever resolved.

As midwives we held a relaxation class each Thursday afternoon for mums-to-be, some of whom were for home delivery and others for delivery at the local maternity home. Among those attending these classes was the wife of a local GP. Troubles were expected as this was her first baby at the 'elderly' age of thirty-five. An urgent request came through one Saturday evening. "Will you come round and convince that husband of mine that I am in labour?" I cycled over to the house as requested.

"Yes, I can see from your face that you are in labour." And a quick examination of her abdomen confirmed my diagnosis.

"Will you ring him? He's at his surgery."

"Just two more patients and I'll be there," was his answer.

Eventually her GP husband arrived, and with difficulty, we got her into the front passenger seat of a rather ostentatious Austin, and with a squeal of the tyres, they set off. I convinced myself, as I was left standing on the gravel drive, that because she was an elderly primigravida, they might just make it to the maternity home. Silence all day Sunday, but on Monday morning from the GP, came an expletive, "Your relaxation classes! She had the baby in the car. We've got a lovely baby boy." I duly congratulated him but deliberately didn't enquire of the condition of the car, knowing it to be brand new with a lovely white interior. However, he did continue to make referrals to our relaxation classes.

My first delivery during the first week on my new district went smoothly, but the second was a very different matter. Fortunately, the husband had given me very clear directions (he was a bus driver) and left all the lights on to enable me to identify the correct house, good forward thinking as the location was down a cinder bridle path and not easy to find.

This was mum's third delivery and labour progressed well until the final stages, but eventually baby Elizabeth arrived. I didn't think my spring balance scales were recording correctly as it was all I could do to hold her suspended in a nappy, and therefore, to ensure accuracy, the kitchen scales with extra weights were brought into use. Twelve- and three-quarter pounds, the largest babe I ever helped into the world! On writing up the notes, I discovered that baby number one had weighed in at eight and a half pounds, and her second at ten and a half pounds. "Your next must be in hospital."

"There won't be another one," was her speedy response.

Forcibly, I reiterated my advice, "But I mean it."

And equally forcibly came the reply, "So do I!"

This was a sentiment I heard often, but was usually very soon forgotten. I wouldn't have accepted her booking for a further pregnancy as baby number four would be considered too dangerous for a home confinement. Had history repeated itself, I think a Caesarean section would have been on the cards. Both midwife and mother were absolutely exhausted. Previous tests for diabetes had proved negative.

Cycling in the dark and driving rain was a great incentive for me to practise my driving. Carrying the gas and air machine within the frame of the bike and held in place by my knees, my rubber macs etc. on the rear carrier and finally my black bag in the front basket, I became quite expert at this circus activity, but was extremely glad when I passed my driving test after just three months. I bought an old but reliable Austin 7 which I garaged a few hundred yards away from my digs, luxury indeed! This was a four-door model which really tested the athleticism of my left foot, as I needed to double de-clutch on changing gears, while remembering not to catch the lights control switch which was also situated in the left floor space.

One night hurrying after a one a.m. call, I was crossing the main road to collect my car when a lorry pulled up, the driver asking if I was OK. I explained my mission. He quickly turned his cab round with his main beam lighting up my way to the garage, and he stayed until I was safely on my way. One of many kind gestures I experienced, but after that experience, when a mum was due I kept my car on the grass verge outside my lodgings. Eventually I sold this car and was provided with the customary Morris Minor, which two years later was replaced by an Austin A30 model, such luxury but I remember not too good on sharp bends.

Several months later, I saw a convoy of horse drawn gypsy caravans making their way through the village of Willerby. One redheaded older lady looked very heavily pregnant, and I was very pleased to wave her and the rest of the contingent a cheery goodbye. The persistent shrill of the telephone dragged me from my slumbers and a voice on the other end said in an indistinguishable accent, "Come quick, she's having it now," and in the same accent gave me directions to the site.

I had never heard of the place so, once my head and car were in gear, I called at the local police station (which was manned twenty-four hours) to get directions. The gypsy had given me the old historic name of Melton Bottoms which the county council had renamed as Ripplingham Crossroads. I asked the sergeant, "Come in two hours and see if I'm OK, please."

"We'll be there," was his reply.

A clear starry night revealed the encampment of horse-drawn caravans on the roadside. A three-legged chair was produced for me to climb between the horse's shafts. Fortunately, no evidence of any horse droppings! I arrived in a somewhat ungainly fashion, to be met not by the redheaded lady, but a small woman in her late thirties. "I'm not due yet," she said, but it was obvious there was no settling things down.

Out of the shadows a young man produced a sooty kettle of boiling water. After laying out my enamelware and precious Dettol, the spare cotton wool, and gamgee square from my emergency supplies (in case there wasn't an accouchement box, a home delivery kit delivered to pre-booked expectant mums), with some difficulty, I poured the water into my dishes only to find a boiled newt. It was fished out with great alacrity. My thought was that at least it was sterile!

Within minutes a tiny baby arrived. No preparations had been made, so a shawl was concocted from the gamgee square and the redhaired auntie's gritty shawl. "You must go to the hospital," I said, which was eight miles away. This baby was far too small to survive the rigours of gypsy life.

Mum protested loudly, "Not the hospital."

Auntie came to the rescue. "I'll go with him." During writing up the notes, I kept one eye on mum and baby and the other on the wooden surround of the fire which was smouldering and kept under control by another family member splashing water onto it. The stable-type door was the only exit from the caravan.

It seemed a long wait but the police arrived as promised, and they radioed for an ambulance. "What are you calling him?" I asked.

"Elvis, yes, 'King of the Gypsies'." Following a speeding trip in the ambulance, the reception sister on our arrival at the cottage hospital in Beverley asked the baby's weight.

"I don't know, he's too small to make my spring balance work."

She weighed him in at two pounds twelve ounces but she did say, "I think he'll make it, get mum to come in tomorrow for further details." During the wait for the police, I had taken mum's obstetric history. She had already three lost pregnancies, her babies in different cemeteries, I suspect clandestinely buried. I suspected Auntie saw to everything.

Having a fairly heavy caseload of general patients, I got up early to visit the new mum who was already up, hair washed and looking spruce, and they were already moving on their way. She assured me, "I'm going to the hospital this morning." I did hear from the Neonatal Unit that she kept her promise and in fact visited her baby regularly.

Two weeks later, a colleague from an adjoining district asked me to stand in for her so that she could accompany her husband to a football match, "I have checked my due ladies and all will be quiet." At about two p.m. a call came in, a gypsy in labour. With clear directions, I found the camp. It seemed to be in the middle of a field of cauliflowers. Half the crop had been harvested (I didn't ask by whom!). This caravan and horse seemed to be set away from the others. "Come in dear." Yes, of course, it was Auntie. The inside of her caravan was much cleaner and the feather bed at the rear was made up with crochet squared blankets.

After a quick examination I said, "You've a long way to go. I'll nip to the shop and get myself something to eat."

"Don't be too long, because I have 'em quick."

"How many?" I enquired.

"This is my tenth." I tried to persuade her to go to Hull Maternity Hospital but she wouldn't even consider such a move. I decided a couple of sausage rolls would settle my rumbling tum.

A voice from behind me at the shop counter said, "Hello stranger." It was the local GP who I had first known as a houseman at Sutton Annexe. We caught up with our news and then discussed my dilemma of the multiparous gypsy. "OK if I come with you? I've never seen inside one of those caravans." Thankfully, he charmingly persuaded Auntie to be delivered in hospital. He had succeeded where I had failed. "She'll get a good scrub there," was his leaving comment. Thankfully no foretold complications attended the birth of her tenth baby.

About a year later I met Elvis and his mum. She was selling pegs and other small items door-to-door. The dirt in the crease of his neck and fingernails revealed that there was still a shortage of soap and running water. Tea leaves in the bottom of his bottle was an indication of his lifestyle, but he was bright eyed, rounded and tanned, weighing I guessed at around twelve pounds. "I've lost another since Elvis," she said. "We couldn't find a midwife. Good to see you again, nurse." With a quick wipe of her nose on her coat sleeve and Elvis still held in Auntie's shawl on her back, she went cheerfully on her way.

The very next day I was called to the wife of a well-known local pop star. The immaculate house had every modern convenience. This was the first fully fitted kitchen I had ever seen. An enamel washing up bowl on an oil-cloth covered table was the usual method of maintaining hygiene, but this kitchen was fully equipped with eye level cupboards and the work surfaces covered with red Formica. An electric oven replaced the usual fireside range, but there was not a table or chair to be seen, a separate dining room being the order of the day. However, I readily adapted to the more modern and plush surroundings, and all was well.

We were taught never to expose a patient. During delivery the blankets were divided, one being folded over on the torso and another on the legs, and thus modesty and warmth were preserved. However, at my first Polish delivery, no blankets were available, just a duvet. This refugee family had duvets on all of their beds (a fashion which would catch on some years later). This was her fourth delivery which was rather difficult. I requested that her baby boy was to be cot-nursed for at least four hours to allow him to recover from his traumatic arrival, rather than being passed around the joyful relatives. On my way home, I realised that I had left the rubber mackintosh sheet in the bathroom. I went back and found Dad singing in Polish and dancing with his newborn in his arms, such was his delight of finally having a son after three daughters. I was persuaded into 'wetting the baby's head' with vodka which had been sent from Poland. In true Polish tradition this was not diluted at all with any cordial, and I have always since refused that particular pleasure.

One of the more difficult cases I attended on the district was one of a sexually transmitted disease. Both husband and wife were infected, and each had independently sought medical help, not telling their spouse. "You treat the wife, I'll treat him in the surgery," said the GP, and so I visited the house during the evening when the coast was clear. I was glad when the course of treatment was completed. I often wondered whether their marriage survived. Presumably, with the level of secrecy involved, each had cheated on the other.

A female GP requested that I do her a favour and take on an expectant mum. "It'll be her third baby and a breech." I pointed out that I had only witnessed two breech births, not having had any 'hands on' experience. "I'll deliver if you'll be at the top end with the gas and air during delivery." This, I agreed to do. Eventually the call came, and on my arrival, the doctor had kept her word and was already setting up her equipment. Mum was very cooperative and I took an opportunity to take a peek at the bottom end. A prolapsed cord cutting off baby's blood supply was always a danger. I pointed to what I thought was a prolapse. "Yes, and she's already got two boys," was the GP's reply. I then realised that the breeches I had previously witnessed had been girls without the 'extras'!

The same GP asked me whether I would like some gauze masks. "Yes, please," I replied. "They're always useful." One of her patients was now a prison inmate and had stitched her some gauze masks as a gift.

"I have got plenty of my own now, but don't tell her about the gift if you ever meet her." I kept the promise.

I was taking my time walking up the path of my next maternity patient, when a local GP screeched to a halt, and shouted, "Don't you know that there's an emergency here?" we both dashed in, and arrived at the side of the cot simultaneously. I grabbed the baby girl, and after whipping off her cold, wet nappy, clasped her to my bare bosom. After what seemed an eternity, the doctor told the mother, "Do what the nurse has done. I'm taking you to Park Street." (children's hospital.)

We propelled mother and baby to his car, and they sped off. A silent prayer of thanks to my mentor and her prompt action with the floppy baby in Liverpool.

After two weeks in hospital, mother and baby were placed in the care of the health visitor.

Within walking distance of my new digs in Anlaby lived a Miss Hall, a retired housekeeper. She had had an enucleation (removal of the eye). Her glass eye had to be removed every evening, and after cleaning, replaced the following morning. This job fell to me as I lived nearby. She was always pleading poverty though her little terrace house was always immaculately clean. Some years later, when 'Danny' came to stay with me and my husband to meet our new daughter, I learned that on Miss Hall's death £1,000 had been found in a blanket chest.

After three years of working as district nurse midwife in the East Riding, owing to my impending marriage, I handed in my notice. I had met my husband-to-be on my parent's farm while he was gaining practical work experience, having graduated from Reading University prior to joining Leeds University staff at their farm in Tadcaster. After a short while he moved to Lincolnshire to support his mother.

Throughout our courtship we had undertaken many trips to and forth across the River Humber on the paddle steamers which ran from Hull to New Holland, a small village on the south bank. This river crossing was always interesting and over time we got to know the ferry crew quite well. Boarding the Lincoln or Tattershall Castle by car, could be particularly challenging, as the pontoon running out into the Humber would rise and fall according to the height of the tide. Getting stuck on a sandbank could be another frustrating hazard of the journey. It was just a matter of waiting for the higher water, but to compensate, there was a bar which sold rather dehydrated sandwiches, biscuits and coffee. Even though there could be the occasional delay, the ferry was still quicker than circumnavigating the River Humber and going round by road via Goole, this being the days before the M180 motorway, and of course, the opening of the Humber Bridge in 1981 negated the need for the ferry.

We were married one Wednesday afternoon in October 1958. Following the luxury of a ten-day honeymoon in Devon and Cornwall, we returned to my parents to collect the contents of my 'bottom drawer' and wedding presents which were then packed into the back of my husband's Hillman Husky. On our first ferry trip as husband and wife, the crew wished us happiness and good fortune. We were not likely to see them as regularly again, but there would still be future crossings to visit my parents on the farm.

Chapter 5 – Marriage and Motherhood

Our new home was in Theddlethorpe, a small village just north of Mablethorpe where my mother-in-law ran the village Post Office and general store. My husband and I had certainly been looking through rose-tinted spectacles when we purchased our first home. The electric cables were hidden behind the wallpaper and there was just one power point, namely a five-amp socket. The water supply was from a well in the garden which ejected brown water, but at least the semi-rotary pump was in the kitchen. The lavatory was an outside privy colloquially known as a 'bucket and chuck it'. Thankfully, when mains water came to the village a year later, we were able to replace this by installing an indoor flushable toilet, as well as having the luxury of an immersion heater.

I accepted these conditions as my husband would have liked us to share with my mother-in-law in her large property, but I had noticed previously that 'Ma' was not 'housewife' trained. I did all the family washing. I had bought an Ada machine which literally danced across the floor when anything larger than a shirt was introduced to the hot swirling water. Each time I baked 'maids of honour', Ma asked me for the recipe.

Her memory must have been short, as she never actually baked any herself.

After three months of being a housewife and getting our house and garden into shape, I was approached by a nurse at the local surgery asking whether I would be interested in working in sick quarters in a civilian capacity at a local RAF camp. Already missing the nursing camaraderie, and after discussion with my husband, I readily accepted the post. "If you can get to the main road, transport will pick you up," came the instructions given by the RAF, so I had the luxury of transport to my new place of work about fifteen miles up the coast, leaving my bicycle in the care of the owner of the filling station on the main road. Not all RAF personnel lived in quarters and a few married men lived in rented accommodation in the area.

During sick parades I kept myself busy on the two small wards, dispensary and dental surgery. Perhaps due to the political climate of the times, the military personnel seemed to be forever on the move, and therefore, their jabs had to be kept up to date. During family surgeries I made myself useful for chaperoning or childcare, and for home visits around the station I had an official car with my own driver.

A rather sad looking young man emerged from the doctor's room. "Are you OK?" I asked.

"No," he answered. "I've got a urachus." I had never heard of this complaint. I later discovered that the urachus is the duct from the bladder draining urine back to the umbilical cord which usually disappears on birth. Whether the medical officer was being facetious intimating that the lad was infantile or whether in fact he really did have an infection tracking down the now redundant duct, I couldn't decide.

During the medical officer's leave, a local GP would stand in, and it was during one family surgery that a French grandma brought in her grandson, her opening statement was, "He's got a cough, I think he's got worms."

"Well before you go fishing, first catch a worm," replied the doctor! He caught my eye and we suppressed our giggles until she was finally out of earshot. "These French have some very interesting ideas," he said, and with a grin, he went off back to his own practice.

The following day, grandma returned. Once seated she, with a flourish, produced a bottle with a silver spoon protruding. "There's the worm!" Indeed, a very dead threadworm was attached to the handle of the spoon, and we had even greater difficulty keeping straight faces.

He escaped to the dispensary, returning with a jar of ointment. "Apply according to instructions. This will catch the little blighters. Check the rest of the family, and in particular, good hygiene after every toilet visit, the eggs are very easily transmitted under fingernails." And with a twinkle in this eye, concluded, "Perhaps the coughing will now cease!"

This episode reminded me of a time on nights on the children's ward. "May I borrow your torch?" had been the request from my colleague. "I'm going on safari." Instructions had been left for every child to be checked for worms, which was much easier to do by torchlight.

After a few short but enjoyable months at the RAF camp I had to leave to nurse my now terminally ill mother-in-law. I knew I had not always been her favourite, but she appreciated my care. My husband took over the running of the family business, and following Ma's death, we were then obliged to move from our cottage into the much larger Post Office with its outbuildings and paddock. At that time the Post Office rule was that the sub-postmaster had to live on the premises.

At the same time my husband's elderly aunt retired from her haberdashery business in Cleethorpes and moved into our old house. Unfortunately, she was not in the best of health and struggled to accept her sister's death. She was very depressed and was also suffering from heart failure – again more home nursing. Not taking too kindly to being the patient, she even doubted my ability of placing her on a bedpan! I asked our local district nurse to call to administer injections required for water retention, as I am sure auntie would have doubted the contents of the syringe! My husband helped me with her nursing as much as he could, especially during the night, but gradually her care was becoming a huge strain on the pair of us. We visited several nursing homes, but I found none which came up to my professional expectations. Eventually, acknowledging my exhaustion, our GP suggested an amenity bed at the local hospital and auntie died peacefully after six days of hospitalisation. Should I have struggled on, I'll never know.

After six years of marriage, we accepted we would not be able to have children. Following simple tests, we had been told that adoption was the only answer to our childless state. We started making enquiries, especially as our local vicar had advised us to 'get a move on'. At that time no one nearing the age of forty was allowed to adopt. He and his wife had almost left it too late but they hadn't even met until their mid-thirties. Happily, they eventually adopted a daughter.

My husband and I successfully applied to the Children's Department of the local Authority, and one Monday afternoon, we received a telephone call from our social worker. "Could I call at five p.m. on my way home?" Later that day she informed us that a three-month-old baby girl was available, and would arrive at two p.m. the next day.

I was suddenly thrown into impending motherhood. Not wanting to find ourselves disappointed, we had made very little practical preparation for the arrival of a child. I only had three matinee coats, which Ma had secretly knitted and hidden, and which I found only after her death. A very good friend from the farm along the road dug out some baby clothes for me that evening. "Keep the clothes, and let me know the minute she arrives," she said excitedly on hearing our good news. She was a true friend, who never let me down and on whom I would come to rely and turn to a great deal in the years that lay ahead. The following day at two thirty p.m. our daughter, Mary, arrived and our family was complete.

The following week I bought a *Women's Weekly* as I quite fancied one of the knitting patterns, but there on the first page was a moving piece of prose by Patience Strong about an adopted child. I took the cutting from the magazine, and pasted it in the front leaf of |Mary's baby photo album, where it is treasured to this day.

My husband and I decided to be open with Mary right from the beginning about her adoption. Even picking her up from her carrycot we would call her our 'chosen one'. As soon as we felt she could understand, we explained further. Living in a village we knew that someone would no doubt delight in breaking the secret if there was one, and if Mary was not aware, then when would be the appropriate time to tell her? We were proved right some years later when a troublesome customer, in front of Mary, mentioned the adoption. Mary answered, "Yes, I was specially chosen…"

We had been advised by our social worker that Mary had some medical problems and an appointment had already been made for her at Sheffield Children's Hospital for the diagnosis of a cyst on her back. Around the same time arriving through the post anonymously we received another prose 'A Child Loaned'. Although we had our suspicions at the time, we never did find out who had sent it (from recent research we believe it had been adapted from a poem by Edgar Albert Guest).

My mother accompanied me on our first attendance in Sheffield. It was 17th December 1964. There had been freezing fog during the night and I remember how silvery-white the trees were, as we began our journey. We arrived on the outskirts of Sheffield, the next task, to find the hospital! I drove around the same traffic controlling policeman three times before finally stopping at this busy junction and asking him for directions. Every visit to the Sheffield Children's Hospital would involve a round trip of one hundred and sixty miles, a journey we would come to know extremely well as the years progressed.

Following an initial assessment, the surgeon advised us that an operation on her spine was essential. After all the paperwork had eventually been signed by Social Services giving permission for the surgery to go ahead (I couldn't sign the consent form myself as the adoption had not been completed), and finally in the following March Mary underwent the first of many operations. On a post-operation visit, the surgeon explained "I did what I could but it was like operating on a jellyfish whilst it's still swimming in the sea. I had to take special care not to further damage the surrounding nerves." He confirmed that the cyst on

Mary's back had been attached to the base of the spinal cord, giving a diagnosis of Lipoma of Cauda Equina and giving a prognosis similar to that of a child suffering from spina bifida. He went on to explain that he would want to see her in the outpatient clinic every six months and warned that her long-term development remained unclear.

In November 1965 adoption day finally arrived, my husband and I, along with Mary attended the Magistrates Court at Louth. The judge had taken off his wig and placed it on the highly polished table in front of us. Mary's one aim throughout the proceedings was to grab the three little curls on the wig. I swiftly diverted her attention, and her endeavours were thankfully thwarted. After some penetrating questions and flattering remarks from the judge, we were told, "Take her home, I know she'll be loved." A bottle of champagne was awaiting our arrival at home, but as it was so near to Christmas, we decided to save this for Mary's christening on Sunday 26th December when we all gathered with family and friends to celebrate a Christmas to remember. At nearly eighteen months, Mary was too old to wear the family christening gown, but had a specially bought warm mustard coat and bonnet.

As well as attending the Sheffield Children's Hospital we were also required to attend the paediatric outpatient clinic at the local hospital, but I was beginning to think that keeping these local appointments was a waste of time as all I was doing was being a cipher relating what had been discussed and decided at Sheffield. After one such consultation, I was almost out of the door when I heard the paediatrician say to Sister, "That child should never have been for adoption."

I dashed back in and asked, "Why?"

"There are homes for these children," was her reply.

My retort, "She has already got a home." I walked out of the consulting room and never returned to that clinic.

Getting wonderful support from all the team at Sheffield was worth travelling the extra miles. As my husband had to stay behind to run the Post Office and shop, my good farming friend who had supplied the baby clothes would frequently accompany me to hospital appointments. I did not relish travelling all that way on my own with a small and sometimes distressed child. To break up our journey we would often stop for a picnic by the canal at Drakeholes, which was a handy and picturesque stop just before the conveniences at Bawtry (the cleanest public toilets that I have ever seen).

From Bawtry we would continue along the A631 through Wickersley and Maltby, and if we had enough time before our hospital appointment, we would stop off at Banners Department Store near the Wicker Arches. They had a wonderful selection of children's clothes and I can particularly remember buying Mary a red coat and bonnet. Other parents would be there buying school uniforms.

Over the years we would see the city centre change, from the opening of the 'Hole in the Road' in 1967. It was so convenient to be able to go from the basement of C&A into Walsh's Department Store on the other side of Fitzalan Square. Mary was always intrigued by the bright lights of the subterranean shops and the fish in the aquarium. With the arrival of Sheffield Supertram in the mid-90s, this iconic landmark disappeared with very little evidence of it ever existing.

Sheffield Children's Hospital, was a world leader in treating children with spina bifida. One of the main medical problems Mary suffered from was that she had continual urinary incontinence owing to nerve damage to the bladder, and any potty training had proved futile. She also suffered from nasty recurrent urine infections, and after four years of travelling back and forth to the Children's Hospital, a radical new procedure was suggested by the consultant to hopefully give Mary the opportunity to lead a more normal life. She would be one of the first children to benefit from this revolutionary surgery.

The name given to this operation was an 'ileal loop conduit' (from the mid-1970s this became more commonly known as a urostomy). The sister on the ward told me that this operation was being performed at the Sheffield Children's Hospital every ten days. They were also planning to catch up with offering this procedure to older children who could now benefit from this pioneering surgery, some of whom had suffered many years of urinary incontinence.

In July 1969 as Mary's operation day approached, I rented a house not far from the hospital. In those days there were no facilities for parents, other than for one breastfeeding mother (there was only one bedroom), to stay with her child at the hospital. My mother stayed with me at the house and thankfully Mary's operation went very well. Around ten days post-operatively she was transferred to Thornbury Annexe (now BMI Thornbury Hospital) for convalescence.

After about a week, while visiting one afternoon, the registrar on her ward round said that Mary could go home the following day. "Tomorrow?" I asked.

"Yes, don't you want your child?" said the registrar, misinterpreting my response.

I quickly replied, "But if she can come home tomorrow, why not today?" Going through my mind was the one-hundred-and-sixty-mile round trip today, to then be repeated the following day. The registrar soon changed her mind and readily agreed, Mary could go home that day.

That July afternoon all the visiting parents had one eye on their child and the other on the television set in the ward watching the Apollo 11 spacecraft returning to earth. I did manage to witness the parachutes open, but due to our speedy exit from the ward with clothes in one black plastic bag and all Mary's toys in the other, we hastily departed and missed the 'splashdown', a fact I am often reminded of when this event is repeated on the television.

The surgeon did explain that as Mary grew she may need further abdominal surgery to reposition the stoma, but such were his surgical skills at the time more than fifty years later, this procedure has not been required. Following discharge from the Children's Hospital our local GP could not understand the complexities of the operation performed and thought that the 'tap' was attached direct to the tummy. He made an appointment to come and watch me change Mary's bags to gain a greater understanding of the surgery and how the stoma was managed on a day-to-day basis.

Anybody familiar with the extensive ranges of disposable stoma products that are available today would be horrified at what was standard issue in the 1960s. We were supplied with three white rubber bags and rubber flanges, together with sturdy woven belts to hold the appliance in place. The rubber bags, which had to be boiled after each use, did not have a one-way valve and urine frequently washed around the outside of the stoma blocking the tap with mucus. A handy pipe-cleaner soon resolved the problem.

Later, as the availability of disposable bags and 'stomahesive' products began to develop, our GP suggested that we should order our needs direct from the suppliers and ask for the invoice to be sent to the surgery. At first all went well, but then the parcels started arriving broken into, with apologies from Royal Mail, though nothing was ever actually missing. I mentioned this to our understanding GP who suggested that with the 'Medical Supply' stickers all over the parcel and the delivery address being a Post Office, it may look as though we were ordering condoms, which possibly made the parcel vulnerable to unscrupulous Royal Mail staff (at the time condoms were considered expensive and so susceptible to the black marketeers). After two requests to the suppliers for them not to put these stickers on, no further vandalism took place!

In September 1969 the time came for Mary to start school. The village primary school had been closed for repairs and for the addition of an extra classroom. The two teachers and children had had temporary accommodation at the primary school in Mablethorpe the previous term, so Mary and another child had missed out on their Friday afternoon pre-school experience. Living less than half a mile from the school (but too far for Mary to walk) on the first morning we had taken her in her pushchair. She was eager to start school but after a week came a request. "Can you take me in the car, please?" She had been teased about riding in a pushchair. I related this story to my mother, and to alleviate this situation, my parents bought Mary a child's wheelchair for her fifth birthday, a lifesaver! (ever-practical Grandma, again).

The headmistress was generally very supportive but when any problems arose, more commonly a leaking urostomy bag, a quick trip home was necessary to change the appliance and put on a new set of dry clothes. On retirement, the headmistress kept in touch with us, usually by phone but also occasionally calling to see Mary, always commenting on how much she had grown and encouraging her academic progress.

My mother adored Mary (their first granddaughter) and she said she would love Mary to spend a holiday with them on the farm, but she couldn't face the prospect of changing the urostomy dressing. "My stomach turns over when I think about it." She then had what she thought was a brilliant idea, she would ask the local district nurse to help. I wrote clear instructions for the nurse on how to change the dressing, and so with two suitcases, one with clothes and books and the other with all the medical paraphernalia, there was another trip on the Humber ferry to deliver Mary for a holiday with her grandparents.

Three days later came a cry for help. The district nurse had flatly refused to visit. My parents brought Mary back over on the ferry to the terminal at New Holland and I arranged to meet them there. Baby changing facilities were not available in those days and so, sitting on the toilet in the 'Ladies' with Mary on my lap I changed the leaking urostomy bag. My parents then returned with Mary on the next ferry to restart her holiday, and I drove the twenty miles back home, feeling rather cross with the attitude of that district nurse.

On many a Saturday morning before nine a.m. Shaun, a seven-year-old pal of Mary's, would walk into the shop asking if he could come to play with Mary. On one occasion we were still at the breakfast table when he looked up and said, "I like toast, Mrs Milner."

"Haven't you had breakfast?"

"No," was his short answer. So we regularly made extra toast and cereals on Saturday mornings. One particular Saturday morning while I was having trouble lighting the sticks and coals on our open fire, Shaun advised me to use hairspray as a propellant.

"Does your mum do that?" I asked.

"No, I do when she is still in bed," was his alarming reply. How we get an insight into other families' lives.

Aged eight, Mary became a member of the local brownie pack in Mablethorpe. They were going on a pack holiday weekend in the south of Lincolnshire. Brown Owl was very caring, and in line with the diversity values of the Guiding movement which remains true today, said, "Of course, Mary comes with us. Pack whatever she needs with instructions and also her wheelchair for excursions." A short holiday with other girls of her own age was thoroughly enjoyed. Brown Owl had no nursing experience, but was willing to learn how to look after a stoma so that Mary could participate in all the activities that brownies had to offer, so very different from the attitude of the district nurse in East Yorkshire.

With two other brownie friends, Mary decided that she wanted to raise some money for children like her who had no mummy or daddy. I discovered that the nearest home for handicapped children was situated at Melton Mowbray, and in light of our local paediatrician's earlier expressed opinions Mary could possibly have ended being one of their residents. The girls decided to have a coffee morning to raise funds for the home. News quickly spread around the village, and before we knew it lots of people were offering their support.

The plans were changed from a coffee morning to afternoon teas, with the final decision to host a 'Soup & Sizzle' evening. There would be home-made minestrone soup followed by either fish fingers, beef burgers or sausages accompanied by chips, and rounded off with home-made fruit pies and cream. Our first fundraising event was very successful, though I can recall that the lovely sunny evening was followed by a descending mist, thus trapping the smell of cooking for over twenty-four hours.

On receiving a cheque for two hundred pounds, which was not an inconsiderable sum in those days, the matron of the home telephoned us to tell us that some of the money would be used to buy a radio which could be controlled by a little boy's tongue, and any remaining money would be spent on facilities for the other children. She did invite us to visit the home but caught up with the busyness of life, we never took her up on her offer although we did continue to support the home for several years with other fundraising events.

About this time, I learnt that Mary's pre-adoption social worker was seriously ill in hospital. Explaining this to Mary, she said, "I would like to send her a card to thank her for giving me a mum and dad." Alas, like all children she prevaricated, and was crestfallen on learning of her death – a lesson remembered.

A few years later our GP asked me to visit a mum to offer support after her little boy had had a urostomy operation. The instructions and guidance she had received from the hospital, were so much clearer than the information I had been given several years earlier, and it was quickly apparent that mum needed no further advice from me as she was already coping extremely well. I was pleased to learn since Mary's operation in the late sixties there had been huge developments in stoma nursing, with a much greater understanding of the level of support patients and their carers need after surgery.

To help maintain Mary's ability to walk and thus her independence, throughout her childhood she required many more orthopaedic operations (we didn't keep count) on her legs and feet, sometimes operating on both limbs at the same time. Recovery from these operations necessitated intermittent periods (varying from six weeks to several months) when her legs were encased in plaster of Paris and she was unable to walk. An NHS wheelchair was not warranted, as between operations Mary was able to walk short distances, and we continued to be ever grateful to my parents for the purchase of our own wheelchair although this did take some hammering over the years.

Wheeling in from play one morning, Mary told me that her pot had broken and indeed there were two large cracks in the plaster of Paris cast. My heart sank; another trip to Sheffield. I rang the plaster room at the Children's Hospital and was told "OK I'll take an early lunch and see you in about two and a half hours." On arriving at the hospital, we were ushered straight through and the old cast was removed (well it virtually fell off). Thankfully the surgeon's handiwork was intact and no lasting damage had been done. A new plaster of Paris cast was applied and we were soon on our eighty-mile return trip. Not quite the day I had originally planned!

It was only years later that Mary eventually confessed that she and her friend had been chariot racing with Sandy (her friend's Labrador) improvising as the horse. All had been going well, until going at speed and seeing a cat, Sandy had taken a sudden right-angled turn, thus tipping Mary out of her chair and resulting in the broken plaster cast.

Although Mary was able to walk, albeit with some difficulty, from about the age of three lightweight aluminium callipers had been attached to her supplied surgical boots. However, as she became more active, these callipers frequently got broken and the welding skills of a local mechanic were frequently called upon. At a routine hospital appointment, the orthopaedic surgeon commented on the welded repairs and asked how the callipers had become broken. I explained that she had caught them when climbing up the apple tree in our garden. "Then we will have to make them from steel, they'll be heavier, but sturdier, she can then swing from branch to branch," was his laughing reply.

In the mid-1970s, the Rowntree Foundation (the charitable arm of a rather famous confectionery group) carried out a survey into the needs of families with handicapped children with the intention of offering additional support to help improve their quality of life. One of the ideas to come out of this survey was to offer musical instruments to disabled children. Mary already had a much-wished-for piano. There was little musical talent in our own family background but my husband and I wanted to encourage any talents she may have inherited from her birth family. I think in time we came to realise this was unlikely to be the case, as our house often reverberated to the not so musical talents of our daughter!

However, one significant problem we were beginning to experience at this time was carrying Mary upstairs to the bathroom (and to bed) when she was wheelchair-bound following surgery. This was becoming especially difficult for my husband owing to his poor health. So, instead of a musical instrument, the Rowntree Foundation gave us a grant towards installing a downstairs toilet with a sliding door to allow access by wheelchair. Perhaps not such a culturally enriching gift, but very much appreciated all the same. An aside to this story is that the village lost its last two-seated privy (no longer used I hasten to add!) as this had been knocked through to the main house to create our new downstairs cloakroom.

On returning home from school one day my daughter asked "Mum, does my swimming costume still fit me? We can go for swimming lessons at Saltfleetby School on a bus during lesson time." The primary school in the next village had the rare luxury of a small swimming pool, complete with changing rooms adapted from two garden sheds (one for the boys and one for the girls). After further enquiry of the newly-appointed headmaster, he flatly refused to let Mary participate in these lessons raising concerns about hygiene. Feeling rather cross I replied, "I can't guarantee many things in this life but she will be the only child who doesn't change the water to a delicate shade of yellow, her urine is locked in a bag." Rather reluctantly, he changed his mind with the proviso that I accompany her. He knew that I was a working mum and I suspected he was trying to put me off, but with a little juggling of my timetable, Mary attended the lessons, learning to swim alongside the other children, a skill I consider vitally important particularly growing up in coastal areas.

Some ladies who owned ponies had set up a local Riding School for the Disabled, a charity championed by Princess Anne. Mary was one of the children invited to join the group. Always ready for new experiences, we accepted the invitation and enthusiastically went along to see what was on offer. The first two or three visits appeared to be going very well, and then there was some reluctance, it appeared that there was always something else Mary preferred to do. On being pressed for answers she exclaimed, "It is just too slow, it's boring just walking around the field and I want to trot!" I tried to explain that the lady had to hold the pony's head and reins and couldn't run round and round the paddock keeping pace with a trotting pony. I think Mary was rather disappointed with my explanation and our budding equestrian decided to hang up her riding hat.

During the mid-1970s, there had been a spate of rather nasty raids on Sub-Post Offices. This understandably caused us some anxiety and we felt that the addition of a barking dog would be a deterrent, as well as providing a playmate for Mary. Our chosen breed was a cocker spaniel as they tended to have deep barks but a friendly nature. Scamp, our new puppy, quickly settled in and did indeed, become a wonderful companion for our daughter. When Mary was in her wheelchair, he learnt to retrieve a tennis ball, placing it into her lap ready to be thrown again. He sulked whenever she was in hospital, almost going crazy detecting her scent when we brought back her clothes to be washed. However, his prowess as a guard dog proved less successful as he was always too frightened to bark when left on his own!

Mary learnt to fly a kite from her wheelchair, but the excitement of flying a standard kite soon diminished, although Scamp always loved chasing the long tail. My husband then purchased a stunt kite for her (these new kites were becoming very popular at the time), rekindling this outdoor activity. With no overhead cables, and a two-and-a-half-acre paddock available, there were no limits to the gymnastics this kite could not perform, and Mary and her father enjoyed many happy hours together.

As she approached eleven years of age, "Where do you think Mary will go when she leaves us?" came the question from the headmaster of the primary school.

"Mablethorpe Secondary," was my reply.

"Oh, I don't think so," was his immediate response. "I have discussed Mary's future with the headmaster there, and it's been decided that she will be going to the school for handicapped children at Horncastle."

On relating this conversation to my husband, we decided to telephone the headmaster at Mablethorpe ourselves enquiring, "What concerns do you have about our daughter attending your school?"

His answer, "We have stairs."

I replied, "So have we. Before you condemn this child, will you please see her?" He agreed to meet with us the following Tuesday after school. I warned Mary that she might be asked to climb some stairs and 'to go slowly and carefully'.

On arriving at the school, we were politely welcomed by the headmaster and indeed Mary was told, "Go to the top of those stairs and see what is there… Are you at the top?… Yes, come down again." He then asked Mary what she wanted to do when she left school.

"Be a secretary."

"I hope you can spell as those typewriters can't! See you in September." Another landmark accomplished.

Many years later I learned that the headmaster of the primary school had enquired of our local midwife (his wife was expecting a child) as to whether there was any likelihood that the new baby could be born handicapped, his reasoning being that he was currently teaching two handicapped children. I cannot repeat my thoughts of this so called 'educated' man.

Growing up, Mary was understandably sometimes frustrated by the limitations of her mobility. While I tried to encourage her to do activities which could be done sitting down, she didn't seem to take after me in my love of needlecraft. A few small tapestries were completed (mainly under sufferance) but that was the limit of her creativity. Interestingly, in adulthood she now enjoys making greetings cards – perhaps a late developer!

Unfortunately, as Mary grew into her early teens further orthopaedic operations were on the cards, with the prospect of her being unable to attend school for several months. I had a word with the education officer at Lincoln and we agreed a peripatetic teacher would visit the house to give lessons once a week. He was very kind and even built a ramp to better accommodate her wheelchair around our house.

As the next term began and Mary became stronger though still wheelchair-bound, a female teacher arrived and taught Mary during lesson time as well as leaving homework to be done in the interim. One day as I was passing though the dining room (school room), a biology lesson was underway involving the drawing of a human thoracic vertebra. On glimpsing over Mary's shoulder, I noticed that the bone was being carefully drawn upside down. I gently pointed out this error suggesting, "Draw it in the way it grows in the body." Later that same day I saw a 'Boots' paper bag blowing around on the lawn. On picking up the bag it was empty but the bones from the biology lesson were strewn across the lawn. Scamp just loved playing with paper bags – thankfully, I think I managed to retrieve all the specimens!

So that Mary would not lose touch with her schoolmates, her form teacher would bring a selection of young people to our house on a Friday evening. Refreshments would be provided, and after a couple of hours of much laughter and merriment, my husband would take them home. We were very grateful to this kind teacher and I think that it was this thoughtfulness that helped Mary assimilate back into school life just in time to study for her CSEs and O Levels.

There was great support for Mary at school, every teacher being encouraging except one, the domestic science teacher. "It's a waste of time Mary doing domestic science," was her attitude although she did allow Mary to stay on in her class working alongside her best friend, Judy. I think both girls enjoyed these classes, from which some lovely dishes were created and consumed.

Examination time came around, and the project for the CSE paper was 'flour'. One afternoon I gave Mary the run of our kitchen and stayed out of the way! A full timed run of the chosen recipes was undertaken (this many years before *Bake Off* was even thought about!) and we enjoyed the resulting dishes for both lunch and supper. The examination day arrived and Mary set off to school with all her equipment and ingredients. She passed the examination with flying colours, being the only pupil to achieve a CSE grade one. To this day Mary enjoys cooking and baking, my particular favourite being her orange Madeira cake.

Mary did very well in her academic achievements gaining seven O Levels. At the prize giving ceremony the following autumn, she was awarded the form prize as well as several subject prizes although, to this day, I am not sure just how she managed to obtain the prize for French! She then undertook a two-year secretarial course at Grimsby College of Technology before joining a local firm of accountants at their branch office in Mablethorpe.

Reaching the age of seventeen Mary achieved another goal – she learnt to drive, a necessity living in rural Lincolnshire. The paddock became a very handy 'race track'!

Photographs

With the farm cat, aged three years

At Sutton Annexe, 1952

Mike with my A-30, 1958

Humber Ferry *The Lincoln Castle*, 1958

Wedding day, October 1958

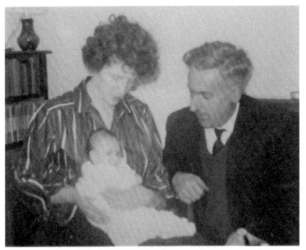

Family complete, 1964

Mary going shopping, 1966 (note the hat and handbag)

Picnic by the Chesterfield Canal at Drakeholes

Five miles from home

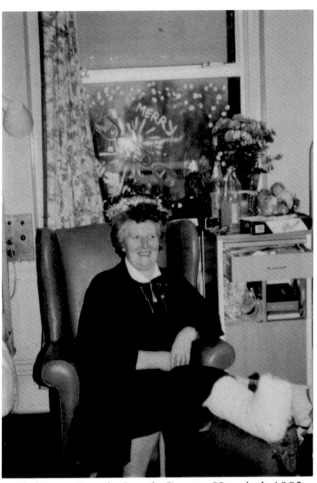

Christmas Day in Louth County Hospital, 1983

Emma in charge of a few lambs

Silver wedding anniversary, October 1983

Retirement and further orthopaedic surgery, 1988

A favourite haunt in North Yorkshire

Egypt with Mary

Mary with the midnight sun

Pre-flight maintenance for glacier flight, Bergen

Dining al fresco, crusing the Med

Cocktails

Back to the beginning – a recent trip to
Withernsea

Chapter 6 – Return to District Nursing

The advent of supermarkets had an adverse effect on small shops and Post Offices. It became necessary to find income from another source. Luckily, when Mary was about three years old, the district nurse who had helped me look after auntie rang me to say that there was a vacancy for a part-time district nurse, and she wondered whether I would be interested. I attended the interview and was awarded the post.

By this time technology had reached the nursing world, and we had an answer machine. The clinic in Mablethorpe where the district nurses were based had once been a seaside boarding house, with its back door opening due north. Our answer machine was installed in the old kitchen, and during the winter the Siberian weather often stopped this machine from working. In the kitchen cum office where the district nurses worked, there was not even room for a single chair, and so all paperwork had to be done standing up! The engineer, who by now was getting regular emergency callouts to our troublesome machine, declared the kitchen was so cold that it was causing the oil in the machine to almost solidify. Finally, it was agreed that we district nurses, together with our answer machine, should be re-housed in our own upstairs office with a desk, chairs and even a gas fire, all thanks to our technological friend.

Time had also brought many other new changes. We now had disposable syringes and needles, plastic aprons and plastic surgical instruments. Gauze and cotton wool was now prescribed by the yard, and although accepted as 'socially clean', the once opened packet was no longer sterile. Our instruments had to be boiled in a pan. The gauze was cut and folded into swabs and the cotton wool torn into fluffy balls. These were then put into a metal biscuit tin lined with white lint and baked in the oven. This was frequently forgotten and often came out in varying shades of brown, but at least they were sterile.

Later on dressing packs were available on prescription and plastic instruments supplied. The patient or relative would boil these plastic instruments but again they were occasionally forgotten, and a melted plastic mess would be apologetically produced – no worries, they were plastic and plentiful. Technically nurses were not supposed to lift a patient over eight stone in weight and hoists were supposed to be used. However, these were in very short supply and stored over thirty miles away, as also were the newly available ripple mattresses.

On her day off a request came from the local midwife who asked if I would mind checking on a gypsy who was in labour. "I can't get childcare and my car is in dock having its service." This time, a pristine luxury caravan was parked in a farmyard. I quickly examined my patient and decided a home delivery was inevitable, as she could deliver even before the ambulance had travelled the six miles from the nearby town, and almost certainly would not have hung on until reaching the hospital fifteen miles away.

Day off or not, I called the local midwife who lived nearby and duly fetched her in my car. The GP arrived from his surgery on a holiday caravan site, and the ambulance was standing by. The labour now seemed to quieten down, and the ambulance men went to the farmhouse for tea and cakes. We three remaining began to 'sit it out'. "I'll do an examination and see what progress has been made," said the GP. "None," was his diagnosis, and he asked for an injection to be given.

"The drugs are at home," said the midwife, and so I lent her my car to go and retrieve them.

The GP went back to his surgery, leaving me in charge. "How embarrassing, I must have lost my touch," I thought. No sooner had their cars disappeared out of the farmyard when labour started again in earnest. Only when the baby was safely nestling in her mother's arms, did I comment on the swiftness of the delivery.

"Well, I wasn't having it in front of all those folk." A truly managed labour, but not by me!

Later during that same summer season, an urgent call came from a guest house. A passing holidaymaker had called in to ask if she could use the bathroom and sadly miscarried into the toilet. Having dealt with the situation and taking her back to her caravan holiday home, I now felt that I had gone full circle, a miscarriage had led me into the world of mums and babies, and happily there had been over two hundred safe deliveries between those two awful events.

District nursing primarily involved dressings, injections and general nursing care of the dying, as well as running baby clinics and doing childhood immunisations (some children came in smiling but more often went out yelling their disgust!). It was around this time that I gained my district nursing qualification. Up until that point there had been no formal qualification for district nurses, the only requirement being to be SRN or midwife trained (a qualified midwife was able to undertake district nursing due to her experiences of working on the district).

The powers that be, decided it was now time to formalise district nurse training. We all attended day lectures and underwent supervision by senior district nursing officers, who would occasionally accompany us during our working day. On completion of this additional training, we were awarded our District Nursing Certificate and thus achieved elevation to the status of Sister.

Each nurse was allocated their own district, but as I was only employed part-time, my main role was working as a relief nurse covering my colleagues when they were either on annual or sick leave. My duties therefore took me all around Lincolnshire, from the coastal strip south of Cleethorpes to just north of Skegness, and inland as far as Horncastle and Woodhall Spa. Of course, over the years I came to know this area of Lincolnshire extremely well.

Whenever a new member of staff who had not already completed their district training joined the team, part of our responsibilities was to take them under our wing, as Nurse Danby had done for me. One elderly lady confided in me that she had adopted her daughter, and somehow she knew that my daughter was also adopted. She begged me to take Mary to see her which, of course, was not really appropriate. However, the following day, I took along our latest new recruit to show her the intricacies of district nursing. On entering the room, the old lady exclaimed, "Oh you've brought your little girl to see me." Ever since then my trainee colleague, and later a very good friend, still calls me 'Mother'. She is two years my junior!

Nurses today have easier access to improving their nursing and medical knowledge, and career progression through residential and day release courses and advanced nursing degrees. Nurses can also choose to specialise in specific disciplines such as palliative nursing or stoma care. Forty years ago things were rather different, and owing to Mary's stoma surgery, my colleagues often asked for advice with stoma care and on some occasions patients visited me at our home.

Lincolnshire is a rural county, and of course, we travelled in all weathers. One summer's day I decided to take two minutes out from my busy schedule. From a special spot on the wolds you could see, stretched out like a patchwork quilt, the red roofs of the town houses of Alford, with its five-sailed windmill and the farmsteads stretching out to the coast. The only blot on the landscape was the North Sea Gas Terminal at Theddlethorpe so I could easily pinpoint our whitewashed home.

On another sunny morning I decided to visit a rather isolated patient via the quieter country route. Halfway along this remote road, I felt the car had picked up a puncture. Cursing my luck, I unloaded the boot to get to the spare wheel when a van of workers pulled up and offered to help me. In what seemed to be a jiffy, they had physically lifted the car up, another man removing the wheel and replacing it with the spare, everything being thrown higgledy-piggledy into the boot. They lightly dismissed my thanks, and we were soon all on our way.

On reaching civilisation I took the tyre to be repaired at a local garage. "No charge nurse," said the mechanic. "One good turn deserves another. You look after my nan and she's so grateful to you for keeping her up to date and sorting her knitting out." Nan was blind and knitted socks on four needles, but frequently came to a halt on realising she had dropped a stitch. I had always admired her flowers which had been given to her on the previous Sunday. On one occasion they were a different variety of daffodils that I had never seen before. Nan passed away, but a year later, whilst nursing another patient in that vicinity, I was given a four-stone brown potato bag, full of daffodil bulbs with a note saying, 'Enjoy, from Nan.'

Relieving another district nurse who was on holiday, I was called to an elderly gentleman to dress his legs. It was a very heavy workload and I didn't get there until around three p.m., working straight through without a lunch break. I was kindly offered a coffee. "Which would you like nurse, Nescafe, Maxwell House or Camp?" I chose Nescafe. "No sugar, thank you." I realised the coffee was sweet, but I thankfully drank it.

I arrived home rather more quickly than I would have anticipated. The following day I visited the old man again and was offered the same refreshment. "Nescafe, please, did you give me Camp yesterday because it was sweet?"

"No, I gave you Nescafe, but I put some brandy in it." A very dangerous thing to do especially on an empty stomach, but thankfully I had arrived home safely. I have since always checked coffee for additional content.

Further along the road lived an elderly gentleman who suffered from leg ulcers. It had been decided his dressings only needed doing once a week. Newspaper was a useful protector on all surfaces and would be later used to wrap up the old dressings to be burnt. Having taken the bandages off, hundreds of maggots fell to the floor. I quickly grabbed a handy tin of fly spray and squirted those wriggling invaders. They absolutely objected to the spray and literally spread right across the newspaper. Quickly wrapping everything up, I shot the offending mess onto the open fire. The only enquiry from my patient, "Has my leg been fly blown?"

"Yes," I replied. "But one good thing they have removed all the dead flesh and you've now got a nice healthy wound."

His quick response, "You'll be using leeches next!" A prophecy? Years later I learned that leeches were now being used again following plastic surgery.

It was Christmas Day, and my nursing list was slightly lighter than usual, so my husband and Mary decided to accompany me on my rounds. During my administrations on one visit along the coast, they walked the short distance to the Humber shore and heard in the foggy distance ships hooters exchanging their usual Christmas greetings.

"He will take some finding," was the opening instruction as I took over a colleague's patch. "He lives in an old railway carriage behind some trees." I duly found the place, but which door? I chose a slightly newer painted one. Wrong, it was the outside loo! After completing his treatment, he asked whether I had a garden.

"Yes, far too big," I replied.

"Tomorrow, bring a spade and I'll give you some of my plants."

"I can't do that, a district nurse with a spade in her car, I've heard of burying our mistakes but that is the limit!"

The next day he supplied a worn-out spade. Its edge was curled after years of use. A rose bush, lilac sapling and an imperial lily bulb (very smelly) was placed into my hands. "My spirit will live on," he said. It was the year of the ladybird invasion. Some swarms were so dense that they turned the trees and bushes red. I had company for several weeks as they slowly crept out of their hiding holes in my car.

A very nasty urine infection hospitalised the old gentleman and he sadly died. Did he know something? The rose bush and lilac died during the next hard winter and spring. The lily bulb survived longer but a couple of years saw its end. "Where is his spirit now?" I ask myself.

"He's let himself go," was the opening gambit from the GP. "Can you go and sort him out?" Yes indeed, he had, too much Guinness and double incontinence, rotting pork chops on the kitchen table and other chaos confirmed the GP's diagnosis. I had to watch where I walked – brilliant idea, turn the clippie rug over, but to my dismay, that had already been done. He told me that cooking and cleaning was women's work but would not pay for a cleaner during his wife's long-term hospitalisation. She passed away, and he was admitted to a local residential home. Who sorted the selling of the bungalow, I never knew.

Before the advent of plastic aprons, we wore starched white cotton ones with square bibs. The bibs were supported by a safety pin or our SRN badges – but I digress. Each morning after meeting up with the rest of our team, I visited Jacob and Bessie (who had just celebrated their diamond wedding anniversary) for general nursing care of Jacob. He was very frail, bed-bound and incontinent. This was an early call if possible. After carrying out the care in the parlour (front room), Bessie always offered a mug of coffee, but due to the early visit, I always refused making the excuse of a heavy caseload and not coffee time yet. But on this occasion I had been delayed by helping a colleague to carry out care on a very confused and obstreperous old lady (we worked in tandem when it was necessary). It was coffee time when I finally got to see Jacob. As I was writing up the notes, Bessie said, "I have made your coffee, it's keeping warm in the oven." She opened the oven door to retrieve my mug of coffee, but this was accompanied by the pungent ammonia whiff of Jacob's unwashed but drying pyjama trousers hanging on the door. How could I upset Bessie by refusing? It was Camp coffee, but at least not in a blue and white striped mug – I drank it!

During the summer months, Bessie baked fruit pies which were always offered to the visiting nurses, but their soggy bottom was often growing blue mould. However, these kind offerings were able to be stowed behind the bib of my white cotton apron – I could just not upset this sweet old lady.

I visited a well-known local matriarch (who suffered from pernicious anaemia) to administer her monthly injection. A four-stone bag of potatoes stood on the clippie rug by the hearth. As she pealed each potato, she threw it unceremoniously into the boiling brown scum on the open fire. This was accompanied by a hiss as the water splashed over the hot coals. The potato peelings in her lap were saved for a family member's pig. Surrounded by her loving but sometimes argumentative family, she certainly was never lonely.

Of course, we travelled in all weathers, which was an absolute delight at times. With views over the Lincolnshire wolds and vast tracts of land towards the sea, it was a pleasure to work in these surroundings. Rarely did we get heavy snow. When we did, the country roads could be difficult to navigate. The weather forecast warned us of the likelihood of very heavy snowfall overnight. In view of this, I drew up the following day's insulin for a rural patient just in case the roads became blocked. The local radio informed us there was very heavy snow and that many roads were blocked with priority being given to the main roads.

I rang the policeman who I knew lived locally to my patient, and learning that the dose kept in the fridge was ready-loaded for administration, he said that he would walk and give the injection. The next day the roads were still dodgy and a local customer offered to accompany me on my rounds. We loaded up a box of ashes and a coal shovel, and off we set. After a couple of miles we found two young men who had come to a halt on the packed snow, their car completely blocking the road. Their only preparation for the conditions was a plastic bag. Spreading the precious ashes, we two women dug the chaps out, and rather embarrassed, they went on their way.

Acting as a locum for one of his partners, the GP asked me to visit a dairy farm about three miles from the surgery to examine a six-month-old baby boy. He was a replica of both his parents who were short of stature and barrel-chested. He was so heavy I could hardly lift him from his pram. On returning to the surgery, I said to the doctor, "He's got a temperature of thirty-eight degrees."

"What's that in English?" he asked.

"Very hot," I replied.

"Did you sound his chest?" he further enquired.

"I can't sound a chest," I responded.

"Any fool can sound a chest."

"Well, this fool can't," I retorted. I did persuade him, however, to do a home visit.

A lunch time check on our friend, the answer machine. "Can you attend a young woman in trouble? Ring me back, I'll meet you there," was the message from a local GP. No further details. This wasn't a young woman but a special needs schoolgirl. By the time we had both arrived she had given birth to a small premature baby (about three and a half pounds). The whole room was in a chaotic state.

"Don't put anything down, you'll never find it again," was his advice. I noticed that the baby had malformed legs and feet. The GP had already radioed for an ambulance as the afterbirth had not come away and the mother needed immediate transfer to hospital. I travelled in the ambulance, with the GP following in his car.

About eight miles into our journey another ambulance met us with a portable incubator, and we carried on to Louth Maternity Hospital with the baby now in the warmed incubator. An obstetrician soon arrived and dealt with the retained afterbirth. He also declared that the baby had a malformed heart. "See one handicap, always look for another," was his advice. I heard later that the baby was transferred to Nottingham and after a couple of days had sadly died. The lodger had made the initial call to the GP surgery and then rapidly disappeared. Suspecting abuse in this case, the GP reported the incident to the appropriate authorities. Thankfully, this was the only time I was involved in a case of paedophilia.

A lighter footnote to this story, the GP offered to take me back as my car was still left outside the patient's house. It was such a smooth ride in his Alfa Romeo car, I felt terribly nauseous and sat with my felt hat in my lap in case of eruptions; luckily, I managed to hold on!

An old chap living on his own was being well supported by his neighbours, accepting meals on wheels twice weekly and other meals supplied from a local residential home the other five days. I was dressing burns on his feet and legs. Due to strong medication, he had fallen asleep in front of an open coal fire, melting the soles of his slippers. Once whilst I was attending to his burns, we were joined by the local GP and a consultant surgeon doing a domiciliary (home) visit. After completing his examination, the consultant stepped aside. I thought that he was going to tell me the diagnosis but he asked, "Is that an ornament or a real rat on the mantelpiece?" It was real enough. "You shouldn't have to work in these conditions," he commented.

"I've worked in much worse," I replied. The gentleman was admitted to hospital, I trust for his welfare, rather than for my working conditions.

"See if you can persuade them to have running water installed," was the parting shot of one of my colleagues as she handed her caseload to me as she was taking a well-earned holiday. The patient concerned was suffering from diabetes, but her home circumstances were certainly not helping her condition. Small in stature and obviously cowed by her husband and son, she had that hollow-eyed expression. When I mentioned the fact of having to go out in all weathers to get water from the tap in the yard, she whispered, "You ask." I did. Running water was installed in the kitchen that same week, but after her death from a stroke, I understand that the supply went back to the yard, something to do with the water rates.

"If you have to carry it, you don't waste it" was the opinion of her husband.

Relieving another colleague going on holiday, I was told about a particular patient. "She seems to be developing new blisters every day; we just can't find the cause of her allergy." On visiting, I was sure that this was not a case of an allergic reaction but a case of pemphigus. During training I had nursed two ladies on the ENT ward at the infirmary with this condition; why on the ENT ward, I never knew. Once having seen the condition, this new case looked very similar. I mentioned my thoughts to the GP.

"Let's get the Bible." (medical encyclopaedia) Looking at photographs of various skin conditions, I immediately picked out pemphigus. According to the book it occurred rarely, only affecting babies and the elderly. "We will start a course of treatment tomorrow," was his response.

"Drop your speed over that bridge, it catches the unwary. I shot through the canvas roof of my wife's sports car and I'm not popular, she complains it is draughty taking the children to school." This was the GP's parting shot after asking me to visit a patient on a remote farm. His advice was forcefully recalled when I left my seat and my air-stewardess-type uniform hat was squashed on the roof of my car. The missing tarmac on the far side of the bridge was evidence of other drivers also having being airborne. On relating this tale, I was asked if I had lost my oil sump? as several other drivers had done so, but on inspection all was well.

Going through the list of another of my colleagues about to go on annual leave, she explained that this gentleman had a very nasty abscess which was discharging heavily and needed daily dressings. On my day off, another colleague had also attended the old chap. "I'm sure he's got a TB abscess." She mentioned this to his GP.

"We will do some more tests." The GP had never seen a case of a TB abscess, although he was the same age as my colleague. While the nurse had been in training witnessing cases of TB, he was still at university and medical school, and by the time he had qualified, sulphur drugs had been developed, with great success. Thankfully we had always burnt the dressings on the coal fire. We three nurses who had attended the patient were then asked to attend hospital for chest x-rays. All three of us were healthy.

On relieving a nurse from a more distant practice, a note was left warning me to blow my car horn on approaching this particular patient's home. "They have a very vicious territorial peacock who likes to attack not only your car but also any visitor to the property, the husband will return the delinquent bird to its aviary." On rolling up his trouser legs, the old man showed me his scars from previous skirmishes. Thinking of birds, takes me back to my Yorkshire days when we fell 'fowl' of a badly behaved parrot. He had had his wings clipped but could scoot across the floor in readiness for attack. He could also swear in three different languages!

Chapter 7 – Village Life (or Post Office 'A&E')

There was an occupational hazard of being a nurse and residing at the village Post Office – people knew where to find you, whatever the time of day or night! Many a time was the comment heard, "I don't want to trouble the doctor, but could you just…? My husband was quite tolerant of this, but he did occasionally go slightly pale at the sight of dripping blood on the hall floor, thankfully a not too often occurrence.

One busy afternoon in the shop a gentleman came rushing in, and pushing in front of the customer already being served by my husband, said, "Can your wife come quickly? My son has got his finger in the chain of his scooter." I was in the office behind the shop and had overheard his request.

"Get back home, I'll bring my first aid box." My first aid box was a redundant metal autoclaving box. This contained a selection of medical and first aid equipment, even a mucus extractor in the case of choking.

By the time I reached the house, the boy, with the aid of his elder brother, had managed to extract his hand from the chain only to find that his little finger had been left behind. I picked up the finger and put it in one of my bowls together with a bag of frozen peas. Obviously, this situation needed a trip to the local A&E Department, and as the family did not have a car, I took the boy and his mum to the hospital together with the detached finger. His only request on the journey was, "Can you drive slowly down the hill, please?"

"Yes," I replied. He was rather pale but thankfully held it all together.

On arriving at the hospital, the casualty officer immediately said that there was no re-stitching of the finger – I had had spent the whole journey with a bowl of frozen peas and his finger on my lap, to no avail. However, the child would need minor surgery to tidy up what was now left of his finger. His mum didn't want to follow us into the treatment room, so it was my job to sit by him keeping him calm. I had previously checked with his mum about his tetanus injections and whether they were up to date. Unfortunately, they were not. He made more fuss about having his trousers down and the injection than the whole previous minor operating procedure. He went back to the hospital ten days later to have the wound checked and stitches removed. The accident was never mentioned again.

One evening a friend of mine who was a ward sister and lived in the village telephoned me to come urgently and rescue a baby from a car which was upside down in a dyke. I knew that the dyke in question was wide and quite deep but thankfully at that time of year held very little water. As I arrived at the scene, the headlights of the car were shining eerily along the bed of the dyke. Fortunately, a neighbour had heard the mum screaming as she had extricated herself from the vehicle. He managed to break the hatchback window, and retrieving the baby from her baby seat, handed her to me.

She was happy and smiling, and after a thorough examination, I was sure all was well, but to make absolutely sure, I advised them to take her to A&E. Mum didn't want an ambulance or the police to be involved, and I didn't ask why. A report came the next day to say 'thank you' and that all was well. She had been reversing out of the driveway and had mistaken the width of the narrow country lane. She had backed straight into the dyke, the car doing a somersault on the way down. Fortunately, the baby had been strapped into her car seat and had been kept safe. Had this incident occurred a few years earlier before child car seats were the norm, I doubt that outcome would have had the same happy ending.

About twenty years earlier I had been called to the same dyke, sadly this time with a tragic ending. In crossing the narrow bridge across the dyke, a child had fallen from her bicycle under the handrail. She was rescued, but sadly too late to save her. I did attend this incident, but was only able to offer support to her distraught parents. Ironically, six weeks after this awful event, and shortly after the death of my mother-in—law, a teenager from the house next door to the bereaved family had gone with a friend down to the beach which was about a mile away, and did not return. Her body surfaced three weeks later very near to where she had last been seen. These two incidents were harsh reminders of the dangers from both the sea and inland waters.

During the Cold War in the early 1970s, the Post Office and shop was deemed the most suitable place in the village for the installation of a warning device in the event of a nuclear attack. A radio device was fitted at the bottom of our staircase, which would be used to broadcast further instructions should it ever become necessary. Test transmissions were relayed at regular intervals to ensure everything was in working order. We were advised of the date and time of these tests, when a code word would be transmitted. This task was often delegated to Mary just in case my husband was otherwise occupied in the shop and missed the crucial code word. Thankfully this machine's intended use was never called upon.

In 1976 a new television programme was broadcast, *Open All Hours* starring Ronnie Barker and David Jason, and supported by Lynda Baron in the role of Nurse Gladys Emmanuel. The programme tells of the ongoing relationships and exploits of a shop owner, his nephew and the local district nurse. This show caused much amusement to me and many of our customers, my husband was less impressed. His long brown overall, which bore a remarkable resemblance to the one worn by Arkwright, was quickly dispatched to be replaced by a shorter grey nylon jacket. The uniform worn by Nurse Gladys was virtually identical to my own. We can only surmise our customers' thoughts, but we in turn could also relate some of our own customers to characters in the show!

One winter's evening having just gone to bed, there was an almighty knock on the back door revealing two distressed local lads whom we had watched grow up from toddlers. One of the lads had come off his motorbike and his friend said "He's a bit muddled, can we leave his bike here?" The 'muddled' young man was left in our care and his pal went home. My new patient was giving me warning signs of concussion. My husband called an ambulance and then went out to survey the scene. A dead donkey was on the side of the road, and with the help of a passing motorist, he dragged the poor animal onto the grass verge.

The police arrived about eight o'clock the following morning to interview us about the incident. We made a special request for them to cover the donkey with some sacks (which we stored in our barn) so that the children going to school would not see the animal. Following the reluctance of the donkey's owner to deal with the scene, my husband eventually persuaded a fellmonger into removing this poor beast. There was at the time a superstition regarding the disposal of donkeys.

Other superstitions believed by some of the older residents of the village related to the treatment of certain medical conditions. One of our regular customers came into the shop asking for my advice. She had been collecting blackberries (known locally as brambles) from the sand hills when a varicose vein had burst. When I took off the improvised bandages (torn sheets), three silver half-crowns fell to the floor. She knew you had to use coins to stem the blood flow, but where to put them had been a mystery to her. I showed her my interpretation – wrap a washed coin in clean gauze, press onto the leaking vein and keep tightly in place with a pressure bandage, the coin need not necessarily be silver.

Another gentleman found his way to our back door. "Now missus, what do you make of that?" A local pig farmer removed his welly boot, and rolling up his trouser leg, to my horror, showed me a very red inflamed blistered leg. "I've got it all over," he said, and on opening his shirt, this confirmed the matter. Wondering whether I dare ask a difficult question and reassuring him that his secret would be safe with me, I enquired as to whether he had got any pigs suffering from erysipelas (a disease found in pigs but rarely in humans). I had only seen one case before, during my nurse training, and this seemed very similar. In that case, the patient had been in a road traffic accident near the cattle market and he had picked up the infection in an open flesh wound.

"By gum, I shouldn't have, I injected the last litter ten days ago," was his reply. I asked him whether he had carefully disposed of the syringe and needle. "I burned it on the kitchen range, but I remember the needle did scratch my leg through my pocket."

"Before you see a doctor, give the vet a ring," I advised. I knew our local experienced GP was on holiday and doubted that his young locum would have ever seen a case of erysipelas.

The next time the farmer was in the shop he said, "You weren't wrong." The vet had indeed confirmed it was erysipeloid (a milder dose of the infection and also thereby immunising himself against future episodes). On advice from the vet, my patient did go to see the doctor who confirmed that indeed he had never seen a case of erysipelas and that the vaccine could well have been the likely cause of his infection.

Several months later two squealing piglets were brought to me by another farming friend. "Can you stitch these, please?" With a curved needle (saved from a craft project) and silk thread (left over from making my bridesmaid's dress), after even more squealing, the job was completed. Unfortunately, one died, its mother had attacked it again.

One winter Sunday afternoon just before we were going out for a rare family outing, there was a knock on the back door. We were only able to enjoy Sunday outings from mid-September through to Whitsun as the shop was open seven days a week during the tourist season. Opening the door, two old chaps from the village were standing there, one with blood dripping from his hand. "Whatever have you done?" I asked.

"I thought I had switched the rotary lawnmower off but lifted it while it was still working, have you got any glue?" The mangled mess not only required glue but lots of stitches, and I also suspected that at least two fingers were either broken or dislocated. His neighbour, who had suggested they call on me, was standing with his back to the scene, and after I had applied a sling to keep the hand elevated, he took the patient to A&E, and we were then able to continue on our planned family outing.

Country life is not always as idyllic as it sounds and there is often a great deal of poverty beneath the surface. Running the village shop, we were perhaps more aware of this problem; our 'tick' book was frequently used but most customers settled their account whenever they could. One particular lady who we came to know very well would certainly fall into this category. She lived with her husband on a twelve-acre smallholding across the fields. Her husband was not a good farmer and incapable of generating even a meagre living from the land. To try to supplement their income she would go potato picking, and nearer Christmas, sprout picking. This was a common seasonal occupation for many women, and although it was hard work, she enjoyed the company of her fellow labourers.

There was no electricity on the smallholding, and while waiting for the agricultural transport, she would enjoy a hot cup of tea and a slice of toast in our shop. At the end of the day, having enjoyed another cup of tea, she would collect a bucket of coal and sticks, which had been given to her by a relative but was stored in our shed (any fuel delivered to her home was likely to be sold by her husband). She then trudged back across the fields.

An urgent phone call came one evening from a close friend and neighbour. Her husband had been doing some DIY, and while using his electric drill, had rather carelessly misplaced the Allen key which was on a string. The drill bit had picked up the string, hurling the Allen key across the living room and hitting his young daughter on the forehead. I quickly picked up my trusted first aid box and dashed down the road. Once the hysterics had settled, thankfully the child was uninjured. I think it was the mother who was more in need of my support.

One Sunday afternoon when I was busy washing shelves in the shop, the telephone rang. "Jackie is in labour, can you come and help us? Her mum is visiting friends in Louth, I've called the doctor and he is coming," (which he did). We both arrived, the doctor quickly grabbing a tablecloth to use as an apron, and between us, the girl was delivered of a baby boy. To my surprise, the doctor flushed the placenta down the loo. I greeted mum, now grandma, on her return. Her shock was palpable. "There will be a wedding sooner than we expected," was her immediate response. I left before any questions were asked.

A local farmer came into the shop one afternoon. "My wife is grumbling, she says that I'm deaf, can you look in my ears?"

After a brief examination I said, "Yes, you've got enough wax to oil your tractor! Go to the chemist and he will sell you some special wax remover."

"SELL, can't you syringe them?"

"No," I responded. "The nurse at the clinic will syringe your ears after the special oil. This oil breaks up the wax which sometimes comes out on its own on your pillow."

A miserable, "Oh, thanks," and he went on his way. I think that having to spend cash was foremost on his mind.

On arriving home from work I was surprised by an unaccompanied bike outside the shop and no evidence of a customer in the shop. On enquiring of my husband, he replied, "I've put him in the kitchen, his welly boot is full of blood." I asked my husband whether he had elevated the leg. He hadn't. "No, it might have trickled out from the top." I went to get my plastic apron and first aid box, and sorting out the state of affairs and applying a pressure bandage from foot to knee, I advised him to see his GP the following day.

"If it bleeds in the night, go straight to A&E." He had previously refused surgery on his varicose veins. Whether it bled again, he kept his own counsel.

We kept the shop open until seven p.m. and this made me a captive advisor. "I've got some dust in my eye, can you have a look?" Moving my patient over to the shop window I asked, "Do you mind me looking here as the daylight is much better." With clean warm water in the undine (a special glass vessel for washing out eyes) and a couple of matchsticks, with a quick flick I was able to turn his eyelid inside out to reveal the irritating foreign body. After a quick wash-out with the clean water and applying an eye pad, I advised him "Keep the eye pad on until you are in bed, if there is any more trouble, see your GP." A quick thank you and he went on his way.

A family (an elderly mother, her son and daughter-in-law and their young daughter) lived in a little cottage, its only access being via a very rough cart track. Their living conditions were extremely basic. Frequently the building's one and only electric light would fail, and candles would be used throughout the cottage. The water from the well was heated on the open fire. The son's main job was to take his wife to and from work, and their daughter to and from school. His mode of transport was a very old Triumph motorbike and an even more dilapidated sidecar. Mum hated her daughter-in-law, but had to tolerate her as she brought home the wages, the only other income being her pension and benefits.

Mother was in charge of the household finances including the benefit books which she would hide, frequently forgetting their whereabouts. On phoning the Benefits Office in Grimsby, my husband was asked whether he could go and look for them. "No," was his short response. Where would one begin to search in someone else's home! After another book had been supplied, she found the original and thought that she could cash both sets of dockets!

Her young granddaughter had never been allowed to mix with other children. She had been due to start at the local primary school for one afternoon a week prior to starting full time lessons, but Grandma had put a stop to this. We had heard on the grapevine that Father Christmas was due to visit the school. After permission from the headmaster, my husband persuaded grandma to let me take the little one to join with the other children to visit Father Christmas. I surreptitiously slipped a little parcel containing a chocolate bar and crayons into Father Christmas's sack. The look of wonderment on her face and the telling of her experience was such a pleasure to witness.

As we were getting ready to go and visit Mary, who was in hospital in Sheffield, there was a knock on the door at seven thirty a.m. Mum, daughter-in-law and little girl were standing there. "Can you take us to my sister? Brian is dead." My husband asked whether the doctor had been called. "No," was the reply. "We've no money for the phone box." My husband drove them the short distance to her sister as requested, and after explaining the situation, left them there to be supported by the family. Shocked, we eventually set off for Sheffield.

Before the funeral, Grandma approached me. "Can I ask a favour, please? We'll be short of cups and saucers for Brian's wake?" I hesitated, I felt that our best 'Royal Albert' might come to harm during transport down the bumpy track to the cottage. Perhaps seeing my reaction, Grandma said, "I don't want to borrow your best tea set, but could I borrow your every-day pots?" There would only be three extra family mourners at the wake but they didn't have enough crockery for their guests. At the time it was more usual for wakes to be held at home and attended by family members only.

On relating this story to my mother, she told me that before the war it was commonplace to borrow crockery and cutlery, for weddings and funerals. The cutlery would have different coloured threads attached, for easy identification, after the event.

There was now no one to take his widow to work or their daughter to school. Social Services became involved and eventually found a 'living-in' housekeeper post for the daughter-in-law and little girl. Grandma coped on her own for a short time, but the cracks began to show when she found out that the daughter-in-law's employer had died. Refusing to return to her mother-in-law, she got another housekeeping job, this time in Sheffield. I'm sure all the upheaval contributed to her having a nervous breakdown and she was unfortunately hospitalised. Her little girl was taken into foster care.

In her loneliness, the old lady became even more confused losing her pension book more frequently. She even forgot how to collect the water from the well. My husband took her fresh water in various receptacles, but this situation could not go on. She had not done her laundry for several weeks, and coal was not being delivered due to the condition of the track and unpaid bills. I rang the social worker yet again. "If you would like to meet me at the shop and we can take some water with us," I suggested.

He went alone to visit her. unsurprisingly, he was denied access. "I will try again in two weeks."

Once again, I offered to accompany him, this time the offer was taken up, and with redundant large sweetie jars we took more water (by now we were running out of suitable receptacles as the water jars were never returned). The state of affairs was much worse than before, but she admitted life would be better in a residential home where her granddaughter would be able to phone her. Her foster parents had been telephoning us to enquire about Grandma, but the calls became less frequent and eventually tailed off. To this day, I wonder what happened to her, I can only hope that she is happy.

Chapter 8 – Nurse Visitor for the Elderly

It is a general misconception of the public that the health visitor's role is only caring for young families. However, this vocation also encompasses overseeing the needs of the elderly population. Owing to the high volume of elderly residents in the Mablethorpe area, as well as a high volume of very young mums, our local health visitor was being totally overwhelmed by her workload. An advert was placed in the local press for an additional health visitor to work in the town, but no one applied.

Lincolnshire Health Authority therefore created a new post of 'nurse visitor for the elderly' which was duly advertised; this was indeed a forward-thinking initiative ahead of its time. "Have you thought about applying for it?" asked my nursing team leader. "You're virtually doing the job already." Although this new role would be full time hours, I would have every weekend off. This would be a luxury our family had never experienced, as during my fourteen years working as a part-time district nurse in Lincolnshire, I had only been entitled to one day a week and one weekend off per calendar month. After a family conference I duly applied. I was interviewed and subsequently offered the appointment.

I was required to attend a residential management course at Lodge Moor Hospital in Sheffield for further training. It was here I quickly learned that I had indeed virtually been doing the job already! I was given a set of weighing scales, urine testing equipment, an auroscope (for examining ears), blood pressure machine and thermometer, a filing cabinet and phone, and I was ready to go. Another luxury of my new job was that I was also given my own small office in the health clinic in Mablethorpe. This rather compact room had previously been the storeroom where we district nurses had kept the incontinence pads, commodes and bedpans! However, as it was also next door to the district nurses' office, I was able to keep in close contact with my nursing colleagues and friends, which was helpful both professionally and personally.

My new role often involved liaising between the local GPs, ward sisters at the local hospital and Social Services. This could sometimes involve rather delicate negotiation between the various professions. The consultant geriatrician had been earlier informed about the new member of the team. He was very welcoming, but straight away referred two of his Mablethorpe patients to me. "Can you visit them unannounced to take their blood pressure?" he asked. "I think one's suffering from 'white coat' syndrome, but the other may need admitting for continuous monitoring," ('white coat' syndrome is a nervous phenomenon often experienced by those visiting members of the medical profession). Today patients are more often encouraged to monitor their own blood pressure using home BP machines.

My patient was grossly obese, and I had never witnessed such a high reading (the upper reading was over two hundred and twelve). "When are you coming again?" I was asked. "We would like to go to Nottingham to see our new grandchild, but we will be back home Sunday evening." I called on the Monday morning, but no reply. I also made several more futile visits. I learned several weeks later that she had had a massive stroke and died in a Nottingham hospital.

Judging by the amount of bungalows that were springing up like mushrooms along the coast, I suspected that the ratio of pensioners to the under sixties was way above the national average. A hint had been shown at my training course at Lodge Moor Hospital that it might be useful to undertake a survey of the population. With the help of the local librarian (he had a copy of the previous census) I compared the figures with Eastbourne – recognised nationally for its elderly population. Percentage-wise Mablethorpe, Sutton-on-Sea and Sandilands came a very close second. I knew at least I wouldn't be bored in my new role!

"Can you meet me there?" was a request after a plea to the consultant geriatrician for a home visit. The allocated time suited him, the GP and me. I went on ahead to explain to the old couple about who the extra visiting doctor would be. A lovely tray of tea and biscuits welcomed us all, and after the examination the doctors took up the offer from her husband of a tour of their beautiful garden; thus providing an opportunity to discuss the situation in private, the decision being for palliative care only. On returning from the garden, the consultant had been given a lovely bunch of roses for his wife. Later a comment from the GP was, "I never get roses for my wife."

"But perhaps you get a 'bottle' at Christmas?" I enquired. I thought I saw a twinkle in his eye!

One January day the weather was bitterly cold and another request came in, this time from the hospital social worker (then more commonly known as the almoner). "Mr Green is asking to go home, but he has been here so long that I am concerned about his home conditions." I was given the key. A neighbour, who I recognised from my previous visits to his wife, spotted my approach to the bungalow.

"There's no heating, the boiler burst due to the frost." I called a plumber, but all he did was to turn the water off and drain the tank. On entering the old man's home, I had noticed the pungent smell of mice; on further investigation they had even nibbled quite a piece from the bar of soap on the handbasin.

I visited the gentleman in hospital a few weeks later and was greeted with, "They've fixed everything and I go home tomorrow." I later discovered that with his Zimmer frame and trolley he was coping remarkably well. I left my phone number with the neighbour should I be needed further but didn't hear from them again.

A visit request came from a local GP. "He says he's got an ulcer. Get what you need from the chemist and I'll drop the prescription in." On removing this gentleman's socks, his only footwear, I found that his toenails had curled round and round and upwards, looking rather like brown garden snails. The one on the fifth toe had penetrated the skin on the side of his foot. This 'ulcer' was easy to diagnose. I arranged transport for him to be seen by the chiropodist at the local hospital (our local chiropodist never had time for emergency appointments). He was horrified by what he saw. After taking some photographs of these rather unique toenails for his archives, he borrowed some cutting equipment from the hospital plaster room. Subsequent follow-up dressings, were done in the patient's home by the district nurses.

Another toenail sufferer was a 'recluse' who only ever ventured out at night. His nails had grown downwards, penetrating the soles of his slippers which were now catching on his threadbare carpet. Due to the old chap's mental state, the chiropodist and I agreed that a home visit was the best course of action. He agreed to visit the gentleman in his own time, once more making use of his camera to take photographs for his records. "How many more of these characters?" he asked me.

"Oh, lots more," I replied though thankfully they did not all need his professional expertise and our local chiropodist could sort out any appointments required.

One day I called unannounced on an elderly diabetic patient, only to find him trying to cut his toenails with a very sharp vegetable knife. I made a quick dash to the nearby chemist for nail clippers! Unfortunately, he had had many of his chiropody appointments cancelled. "I've given up on our local one," he told me.

"With your condition, you really must keep on trying," I encouraged. Somehow, I think he would now keep his independence with the use of his lovely new nail clippers.

A few weeks later I visited another diabetic patient who had just completed an attack on his toenails, this time with wire cutters! Not only bonsaing his toenails but also the surrounding flesh; a preventive course of antibiotics, light dressings and exposure to circulating cold air happily saved him from the likelihood of gangrene. Good foot and leg care is essential for diabetics.

One morning a lady popped into the office. "I've come to see you. Mother has got an awful rash and it's very sore when she passes urine. We've got cream from the chemist but it's useless."

"Let me finish this paperwork and I'll call in about thirty minutes," I replied. I had convinced myself that the old lady was suffering from a urine infection and so had put my urine testing equipment in my pocket. However, once a sample had been provided by my new patient, I discovered there was no infection but that the reading was 'off the scale' for sugar.

"I'm afraid you've developed diabetes," I explained.

"Yes, I know, I take tablets for it." I then noticed a bottle of Lucozade on the dressing table.

"Mum's quite addicted to it," said her daughter. The high glucose reading was suddenly explained. I rang her GP from their home and he agreed to send her to Louth Hospital. After a two week stay, she was home again, her daughter having learned how to administer the insulin injections. The rash and soreness had gone and mum was back to her usual happy self.

Coming out of the chemist shop on the High Street I was approached by a lady who told me that the warden of the new flats around the corner was having to night sit with a resident, and asked if I could help the warden in any way. My first thought was whether this could be a case for the Marie Curie night sitting service, and asking myself why the district nurses had not already been involved, I immediately called to see the warden, who accompanied me to see the patient who was indeed very poorly. "We don't know what's wrong with her but she should be going to Majorca tomorrow." Her suitcase was already packed in the bedroom. The usual urine tests were clear but her blood pressure readings were erratic, and I was baffled; none of her symptoms made sense to me.

I called into the surgery to see her GP who said that he had already had a call from the warden. "What do you think the problem might be?" he asked.

"I really don't know," was my reply. He ordered an ambulance to take her to Louth Hospital, and after two days she was transferred to Grimsby where she died from a ruptured aortic aneurysm.

After a discussion with the GP and local housing officer, an elderly man had been rehoused from his lonely caravan, but unfortunately his mental state had seemed to suffer as a result of this kindly intervention. He was convinced that his new neighbours were spying on him, so he always kept the curtains closed, and in his confusion, he kept altering the timing on his central heating, usually to the 'off' position. His explanation was that electricity was too dear. He would not answer the warden's call but remained silent. "Do at least acknowledge that you are OK," he was asked, but this request fell on deaf ears!

I asked the housing manager if the old fireplace could be reinstated, but before this could be done (this involved lots of paperwork) the patient had lit a camp fire on the floor of his living room. The GP and I persuaded the consultant psychiatrist to undertake a home visit. An attempt was made to interview the old chap through the letterbox as our patient refused to open the door. Silence again. "We'll try another time," was the only response and help from the psychiatrist. His neighbours continued to keep an eye on him from a distance and several weeks later, after he had not been seen or heard for three days, the police were duly called. The old chap had sadly passed away, but in his shopping trolley, was found over £1,000. So much for saving on fuel!

"Do something for that woman." She had lit a bonfire in her front garden burning a mattress and other soft furnishings, the acrid smoke crossing the road and enveloping the local doctor's house and surgery before the fire brigade arrived. She was of indeterminate age, though I suspect she was in her late forties. She suffered from urinary incontinence and was also trying to look after her teenage handicapped son who was permanently wheelchair-bound. I arranged for a supply of incontinence products to be delivered and a referral was made to a consultant gynaecologist for further assessment.

With safety in mind, I suggested she remove the piles of newspaper and other detritus from the hallway, advising that she would not be able to get her son's wheelchair out of the front door if there was a fire. In her efforts to overcome this difficulty, she just removed the door and surrounding frame, and then proceeded to widen the gap even further by removing a couple of rows of bricks but leaving the brick rubble in the hallway, thus creating even more hazards than before!

Surely this family situation was a case for a referral to Social Services, but unfortunately, she did not meet any of their criteria to receive help. She was not certifiable, nor was her son a child. I did manage to arrange some day care for her son at a local residential home, and the son of a local policeman kindly agreed to take him daily back and forth in his wheelchair. I rather think the elderly residents of the home became very fond of him.

A short time later, a case of fraud was brought against his mother, and she was unfortunately handed a custodial sentence. Her son was then taken permanently into care. Following completion of her sentence, she was released from prison and brought back home by prison transport one Friday afternoon and left outside her house without a penny to her name. In the interim, unbeknown to her and presumably not checked by the prison authorities, her house had been repossessed and was now boarded up.

Our paths just happened to cross in town later that Friday afternoon. She had attempted to contact the local Social Security Office for emergency help, but by this time on a Friday afternoon the office had closed for the weekend. "Sister," she said. "I'll get by somehow." I couldn't bear to think that she would go hungry over the weekend, and so I dropped the price of two fish and chip suppers into a local fish and chip shop. She was very grateful. The chippie owner and I were her 'best friends'. I went round to check on her first thing Monday morning, to find her house still boarded up.

She told me the fish and chip shop owner had given her a blanket and candle (she was petrified of the dark) and that she had spent Friday night in the outside toilet. In her desperation, the next day she had removed some of the boarding and climbed back into her old home. I climbed into the house to talk to her, but upon the realisation I too was now trespassing, quickly climbed back out again. However, she did tell me she thought she had found some digs in the town so we went our separate ways with the offer for her to contact me again if required.

Sometime later I heard that she had been evicted from the boarding house for wetting the bed – I was sad that she had not sought my help further. I understood she had moved out of the town and unfortunately, as I did not know where she had gone, I was unable to refer her onto my colleagues for follow up. Sadly, I suspect her story was not an isolated case.

I received a call in my office from London. "Can you help my mother? She is eighty-nine and is exhausted." This desperate call got cut off, but fortunately I had at least acquired mum's address. I duly went round to visit her; she was surprised to see me, but very welcoming. She walked with a stick and looked frail and fragile.

Her question, "Can you tell my lodger how to deal with his colostomy?" took me rather by surprise. "He comes in drunk and he is not applying his bags properly, and tell him to stay away from the pub." I arranged to visit again the following day to show him how to manage his colostomy.

When I arrived as promised, the lodger had a hungover expression and didn't really understand, nor did he want to know, how to properly deal with his colostomy. "But you must have been shown how to deal with your stoma when you were in hospital?" I informed him.

"Can you come every day to change it for me?" was his response.

"No," I replied, "I've shown you how to do it."

"Well, if you won't come, I'll ask the district nurse to come and change it instead." Yes, I guessed, he really did not want to be bothered to change his own colostomy bags. I had heard about this type of situation before. From my experience it appears that men struggle more often than women with adapting to living with a stoma.

His long-suffering landlady was carrying coal up to his bedroom fire, cooking all his meals and doing his very dirty washing. Knowing that her lodger was terminally ill, I contacted the hospice in Lincoln. He was then visited by one of their doctors who promised him a bed for ten days. With this respite in place, I telephoned the lady's daughter in London who agreed to collect her mum to give her a holiday. Sadly, I later learned that she had passed away at her daughter's residence two weeks later. On discharge from the hospice her lodger was found a temporary bed in a local residential home but he still insisted on getting drunk and becoming incapable. He was later readmitted to the hospice where he peacefully died.

I used to telephone one of my elderly, confused patients each evening to remind her to take her tablets which were placed in the eggcup on her mantelpiece. One evening there was no reply, perhaps she had gone to bed early I consoled myself. But I was wrong in my assumption. The local GP phoned me about nine o'clock. "Can you come and look for Jessie," he said. "She was last seen walking in the sea accompanied by her budgie in its cage; she'll relate to you. Keep a low profile and put your wellies on."

With my husband and daughter in one car and me in my county work car we set off on the short drive into Mablethorpe. We found her walking in the town, very wet and still with her budgie in its cage. I picked Jessie up, along with her feathery companion and took them both to a local residential home. It took me two and a half hours before she could be persuaded to get into bed. A permanent resident of the home was the owner's cat who was very interested in the new feathered arrival, and so was quickly removed to the kitchen. The home owner had a very restless night trying to settle Jessie down; in the end she had pushed a settee in front of her bedroom door where she had slept, just in case there were further thoughts of going for a paddle!

I was late the next morning, having only found my bed in the early hours followed by broken sleep. The GP had cajoled a social worker to attend a meeting regarding the future care of our somewhat confused old lady. Attending this meeting I soon realised that we weren't getting anywhere and the problem was to remain ours. In desperation, I said to the doctor, "Next time you have a nocturnal 'paddler', call the social worker, not me." Surprise, surprise, a specialist residential home was magically found within half an hour. Her relatives informed me that she had happily settled into her new abode and was enjoying the company of the other residents and staff. She also enjoyed washing up and other light domestic duties. I didn't ask about the budgie as we certainly did not want a new pet, as Mary was petrified of flying birds.

I suspected that there was an ulterior motive for being invited to coffee by a local GP. We were to meet in the coffee shop next door to the chemist. He was actually on time! Morning surgery usually ran over as it was a matter of 'first there, first seen', no appointments necessary. Rather enjoying a second cup of coffee, in a low voice I hardly dared enquire of the reason for our meeting. Yes, indeed there were two new cases, both women.

"I'll go with you now, and introduce you." Her son, a well-known local bachelor, was struggling to care for his mum. She didn't want a nurse bossing her around (the chance would be a fine thing!). We found our patient lying in the middle of a four-poster bed complete with threadbare curtains and a leaking feather bed and eiderdown. The room looked as though several chickens had been plucked already. On our family visits to stately homes we had seen various four posters, but I had never seen one occupied! I shook hands with the old lady and told her I would get one of my special nurses to care for her, and her son agreed. Later, out of earshot, her son also agreed to accept some home help with cooking and cleaning the rest of the house. From the smell, I suspected that the numerous cats didn't always go outside to relieve themselves.

I sought out one of my old colleagues. "Don't blame me," I began, as I warned her that this was a difficult case and that the doctor should have really referred her himself. Her nurse would need long arms and legs in order to even reach the patient in her bed. Fluffing up a feather bed with the patient still in it was difficult and tiring, but few patients got bedsores. They borrowed one of my porcelain invalid cups from my collection (a hobby of mine) as she didn't like the plastic ones, and upon her death the cup was duly returned. With its pretty design, I remember her each time I move that particular piece of crockery.

My GP colleague's second request as we drank our coffee was, "To sort that woman out, everyone is complaining about the stink." I duly visited my new patient at her home and found an intelligent middle-aged woman living on her own with one cat for company. She had suffered polio as a child and was permanently in a wheelchair. It was quickly apparent that her housekeeping skills were non-existent. Her ulcerated legs and feet were beyond recognition. It was difficult beyond words to breathe; in fact, the smell reached beyond the front door.

She had been employed in a responsible position, but not surprisingly, this had ended by mutual consent. Employed by the home help service at the time was one big hearted care worker whom I knew from my nursing days, and I knew that she would sort her out. She had extra pay for taking on difficult cases. "I'll fix it with your supervisor, but can you do something?" I gave her a supply of paper masks, plastic aprons and disposable gloves and also a 'helping hand' tool which was very useful for the wheelchair bound, and also for the carer in helping to remove all the detritus from under the bed, and around the ground floors.

On putting in a request for the district nurses to visit for treatment to her legs and feet, they moaned, "We've heard of her." They did attend to treat her legs and feet; purchasing shampoo, they finally persuaded her to have a chair bath and her hair washed. Despite all our efforts, eventually she became extremely ill and was admitted to hospital. She had an amputation of one of her legs and after convalescence was able to return to her own home, where she continued to live for a good many years. However, her hygiene never improved. She had a little invalid car which she used to visit our village shop, tooting her horn to be served by my husband on the pavement. He always carefully put her money in a separate compartment to be cleaned later. The district nurses and I were never forgiven for our interference but she did allow them to continue dressing her remaining leg and foot.

It was during my weekly visits to the geriatric ward at the local hospital that we could organise respite care for those families taking care of elderly relatives. This always had to be booked ahead for the time needed, and one particular old lady looked forward to her fourteen-day stay, each year. "Please don't tell her we're only going away for ten days but we would just like two weeks on our own," came the plea from her family; this seemed such a minor request after independently and diligently caring for her for the other fifty weeks of the year.

"We used to come here as children, young lads with old prams and pushchairs would meet us at the railway station, load up our suitcases, and after finding out the location of our holiday digs, would charge accordingly; in fact, we had our honeymoon here. When we saw this bungalow for sale we decided to retire here, the pity is that my husband didn't live long enough to enjoy our retirement." This is a version of many of the stories related to me.

"We have a team of volunteers raising money to get a day centre in Mablethorpe, would you like to join us?" I encouraged my new patient. After hesitating but with a little persuasion, she agreed to help sell raffle tickets. This proved a very beneficial outcome for us all. She joined the fundraising team and became an energetic helper when we reached our goal and the day centre was opened. She enjoyed the home-made lunches and was always eager to serve the cups of tea and coffee.

I was just completing my visit to a newly bereaved widower who was having difficulty controlling his diabetes, when he asked me whether I knew of a 'deserving poor' woman who would accept his deceased wife's clothing. He had already packed two suitcases but wanted the clothes to be distributed out of town. I didn't need to scratch my brain too hard to think of a suitable beneficiary and he helped me load the suitcases into my car. On reaching home, our 'potato picking' friend was in the shop and I enquired as to whether she would like some warm clothes. She gladly accepted but asked if she could collect them in small parcels so not to draw attention to these gifts.

Not long after this event she decided to leave her husband. With the support of our local vicar and a social worker, a meeting was arranged to be held in our lounge, and immediately following this meeting, she was rehoused with a friend in the village – she never went back to her home. I was later called to be a character witness at the Magistrates' Court as her husband would not co-operate with the authorities regarding his income. He was classed as 'self-employed' although it had been his wife who had purchased his weekly National Insurance stamp. After much legal debate between the solicitors and the chairman of the bench, maintenance was agreed at five pence a week enabling her to access full benefits minus the five pence. She eventually moved into a flat above a cafe where she was employed washing up, and was very happy. Sadly, she was only able to enjoy the comforts of her new lifestyle for a few short years.

A husband called into my office saying that his wife was becoming more muddled. I visited the couple, taking along my equipment. I discovered that not only had she a raised temperature but a nasty urine infection. A course of antibiotics seemed to sort this out, including her muddled state. Urine infections can often cause confusion in the elderly. Quite a few patients were presenting with insomnia, depression and other signs of distress. Some took up the offer of day centre care one day a week.

So many elderly residents of the town were very lonely, especially during the shorter days and longer nights of the winter months. A familiar story from their offspring, who very often lived in the Midlands, was that they were very busy and couldn't possibly find time to visit their parents, but somehow, they found that it was more convenient to pay a visit during the summer months!

"I'm not paying that!" was the response from a resident of a large coastal mansion when I suggested that his wife, Molly, go into a residential home. Molly was suffering from severe dementia, and as her sole carer, he was really struggling to cope. On one repeat visit I arrived to find this gentleman as he was being loaded into an ambulance following a suspected heart attack. His parting shot to his onlooking neighbours was, "Look after Molly for me." He was subsequently admitted to the coronary care unit at Grimsby Hospital.

After a few days, the caring neighbours, doing their best, were finding the pressure of rescuing Molly from her night-time excursions too stressful. I called the social worker, who took Molly to see her husband in hospital as she could not be persuaded that he was ill. Seeing him in hospital she was finally persuaded that he was indeed very poorly, and with some coaxing from her husband, she finally agreed to go into a care home. This was the last time she would see him; sadly, he passed away three days later.

Monday 20th November 1983 started off as a pretty routine day; little did I know what lay ahead. I left my office late afternoon to visit an old gentleman in Theddlethorpe as his house was on my way home. Acknowledging the local ambulance crew in the ambulance station (which was next door to the clinic), I duly wished them a quiet evening and set off for my final visit of the day. Unfortunately, I was to see them again only too soon.

On a rather difficult bend in the road on which I must have travelled many hundreds of times over the years, a female drunken driver recklessly drove her powerful Triumph car head-on into my little Ford Fiesta. As one can imagine, the front of my car caved in quite badly trapping my feet under the pedals, and leaving me and my car in a precarious and dangerous position on the road. Thank goodness for seatbelts, or things could have been so much worse.

The pilot of a helicopter on a returning journey from the North Sea rigs saw the situation and he took an unscheduled landing in the field where the drunken woman's car had ended up. This worried me as I could only think that the driver had suffered more serious injuries. However, this was not the case; she had simply run away and abandoned me.

The first vehicle on the scene just happened to be one of my neighbours driving home from work. Seeing my obvious predicament, he quickly summoned help from an adjacent house and directed traffic safely around the crash site. A blue-light ambulance soon arrived and I was once again face to face with my ambulance colleagues. I think their friendly chit-chat was actually to determine whether or not I had suffered head injuries; no, I could recall every minute – the noise of the impact had been tremendous.

On coming round from the anaesthetic, the casualty officer warned me that although he had done his best to repair the damage to my leg and foot (a compound fracture with dislocation of the ankle), he could not guarantee that I might not lose my left foot. This was not the best of news to hear.

I was in hospital for seven weeks, and during that time, the patient I had been planning to visit on my way home, was admitted onto an adjacent ward suffering from heart failure and confusion. A kindly nurse took me in a wheelchair to see him. He recognised me, realising that I had been on my way to visit him when I had had my accident. Later, it was only enquiring of the ward staff that I had found out he had died peacefully four or five days later. Sadly, he would not be performing his duties as Father Christmas at the village school ever again.

After six months' sick leave on full pay, followed by a further six months, at half pay (as is the usual contractual agreement for NHS employees), I was still not well enough to return to work and was requested to visit the Occupational Health Department. The doctor who examined me decided that I was no longer able to continue in my working role and recommended retirement on the grounds of ill health.

This was not the way I would have wished to finish my nursing career.

Chapter 9 – Retirement – part one

Following my enforced retirement, with me still needing crutches, my husband and I struggled on with the family business, but finances were becoming increasingly difficult. The income from the shop was slowly dwindling as more supermarkets opened in Mablethorpe and the surrounding area. However, one gleam of light was that the caravan site was becoming popular. Many of our campers and caravanners not only paid their site fees but also made purchases from the shop thus helping to just about keep the business above water.

My husband had started our 'sheep farming' a few years earlier by taking in two neutered Soay sheep (the breed originated on the island of Soay off the west coast of Scotland, but our pair came from Mablethorpe Zoo!). Because of innate ability to jump over any fence they were always housed in the barn overnight. During one of their escapades, they had managed to cross two fields, scaling barbed wire fences and leaping across water filled dykes. By the time three men and a dog had managed to recapture them, they had reached the main road on the other side of the village. Following this particular incident, we were recommended to get an electric fence which proved invaluable. After a couple of weeks, the fence was switched off, they had learnt their lesson putting paid to any further ideas of freedom. By now our flock had grown to include a few Jacob sheep, who all responded to the name 'Emma' and a bucket of sheep nuts. The baby lambs were an additional attraction in the spring.

We had registered our camping and caravan site with the Camping and Caravan Club, and unbeknown to us, the site had also been advertised in a Dutch tourist guide. Over the years we welcomed several continental holidaymakers – somehow we always managed with our 'schoolboy' French and a rather strange version of charades! Thirty years later, and after two house moves, a Dutch couple still call at my home always bringing lovely gifts, usually cheese or tulip bulbs, the resulting flowers in the spring are a lovely reminder of their visit.

My husband and I decided that we desperately needed a holiday. We managed to find a relief manager who could do the day to day running of the shop and Post Office, but we had to be back on the Friday evening as the weekly balancing of the Post Office books was too complicated for her to manage. After a couple of weeks back home from our holiday, the sewer became blocked. Our friendly handyman (who took Woodbine cigarettes as payment) informed us that the cause of the trouble was a baby's nappy. "Didn't you know that your house was turned into a hotel?" He explained that no sooner had our car disappeared down the road, our relief manager's extended family had (without our knowledge or permission) moved in making full use of our large property for a seaside holiday of their own. We promised ourselves that the good lady would not be employed again, but unfortunately this situation did not arise as sadly this proved to be our last holiday together.

My husband's health was steadily deteriorating. He had suffered pneumonia as a toddler and was always 'chesty', the condition now known as COPD. I persuaded him to go to the surgery. Our GP telephoned me to say he would like to send him into hospital and ordered the ambulance to the surgery. Unfortunately, while in hospital, he suffered a massive stroke and died peacefully. We had been married just over twenty-six years. We had at least celebrated our silver wedding anniversary with a party for friends and customers a few weeks prior to my road traffic accident.

There was little or even no sympathy from Post Office Headquarters. Their first question was, "Are you selling up?"

"No," I replied. I had already decided to stay on and carry on with the business. I had always advised my newly bereaved clients to stay put if possible for at least a year before making any major decision. I took my own advice.

My cleaning lady was a great help with the housework, but I also decided I needed some extra help in the shop to cover my absence while I made the weekly run to the warehouses in Grimsby to replenish stock. A friend and close neighbour was happy to be employed on a Wednesday afternoon when the Post Office section would be closed. On my return from the warehouses other neighbours could often be found helping unloading the car and restocking the shelves. I really don't think I could have managed during this time without their help.

Two weeks before Christmas 1986 Mary was made redundant from her job at the accountants. Her employer had decided that they would downgrade their office in Mablethorpe to part time. Mary's redundancy was a blessing in one way, as she now had more time to help me with the books and VAT returns, but a village shop was no future for a teenager. She decided that she would like to retrain as a medical secretary, but the only course available was at Richmond College, Sheffield. She applied and was accepted for the course beginning in September. After her course she accepted the position as medical secretary at a large GP practice on the outskirts of Sheffield, where she still works today.

Looking after the Post Office, shop, sheep and the caravan site was becoming onerous. I consulted a friend of my husband, a local sheep farmer, who had helped me with my small flock after my husband's death. "Sell them," was his answer. "They're too much for you; I'll fix it and arrange with the market." On the appointed day a tractor and trailer took them all to Louth Market – a sad but sensible decision. When enquiring of the costs of transport I was told "It's free, it gave us a morning out."

My foot and leg were getting worse. A suitable bungalow in the village came up for sale, and I realised that, yes, I had earned my retirement, and sold up. A wonderful surprise retirement party was held at the village pub where villagers presented me with a lovely barometer. It is still accurate today, and as it hangs on my lounge wall, it brings back happy memories of village life in rural Lincolnshire.

Chapter 10 – Retirement – part two

Having once settled into my new bungalow, I was approached by the chair of the school governors to see if I would consider becoming a governor at our local primary school which Mary had attended. He assured me that the post was not too onerous. I accepted, and after a year I was appointed chair myself with the proviso this would only be a short tenure. I found the rules and regulations of the Education Authority not too dissimilar to the NHS, wading my way through the budget and staffing issues, including the appointing of a new head-teacher. The successful candidate soon settled in, and together we would attend local meetings of chairs and headteachers, gaining further insight into the running of schools.

I answered a knock on my front door to a neighbour whose job had been caring for new offenders. "Have you seen the advert from Social Services for visitors to inspect residential homes, I've thought of answering, how about you? You would know what to look for." I thought this over and together we attended a meeting with other volunteers. Sometime later, I received a call from Social Services asking if I would meet with a social worker at a local residential home (I had previously informed them that I would not inspect homes managed by people I had previously worked with).

The homes I visited were all warm and comfortable. I would talk to the residents and ask whether they were content with their surroundings. I remember at one home, on looking into a spare empty room, the male social worker commented that the handbasin would need replacing. From experience I could see that it had previously been used as a urinal, a good clean with a household product containing limescale remover, would return the basin to pristine condition. I suspect some of the male residents had found the empty room more convenient than the longer walk down the corridor to the bathroom!

I also found out that on Fridays they preferred fish 'n' chips from the local chippie, and an ambulant resident would take pleasure in collecting the order for lunch.

The usual term for voluntary inspectors was three years, however, I was asked to stay on for a further year. I had enjoyed travelling along the old familiar roads from my district nursing days.

I thought that my professional career was over. However, I was approached in the local Co-op car park. "Could you help us out as relief night sister just for one night a week, please? The main duties will be giving out medication and the tea trolley in the morning – we'll provide the uniform." I initially hesitated but was persuaded to accept the post, so my navy-blue belt and silver buckle were retrieved and another chapter began.

A request came from the housekeeper, "If you've got time, please can you put the sheets and pillowcases through the rollers?" We rarely got time! It frequently took three of us to help patients to the bathroom, and making extra night-time drinks kept me busy. A special request on Christmas Eve was, "Please can you put the turkeys in the oven at four a.m.?"

My arthritic hip was giving me a lot more pain – it was due for replacement. I was on duty the night before going into hospital for the operation, and a comment from one of the nurses on the ward was, "You do sleep well!" At least it spared me any pre-operative nerves. After six weeks' recuperation, the owner of the home asked if I could help out again. The answer this time was a definitive, "NO!"

Unfortunately, a short time later on early morning waking, I realised something was wrong and I was in the early stages of having a stroke. I immediately called the 'out of hours' doctors service, and a GP soon visited confirming my fears. It was during hospital admission that I gave my notice as chair of governors, as I realised, I would probably not be able to return to the role – an unexpected ending to another chapter of my life.

During one of my outpatient appointments following my stroke, my consultant asked me whether I would be a patient representative on the hospital stroke committee – I thought that this might be interesting and

I attended my first meeting the following month. An insight into the modern techniques and treatments of post-stroke patients was an eye-opener. We had discussions with the consultant, ward sister, physiotherapist, occupational therapists and the community support worker – so different from my early nursing days.

At one of these meetings I was asked if I would consider setting up a stroke club. I took the thought home and contacted the Nottingham Stroke Club, but soon realised that this would be more onerous than I had first thought. Louth County Hospital has a large rural catchment area with extremely poor transport links – in fact even at that time some villages were only serviced by the Post Office bus. As very few post-stroke patients could drive, there would be a dependency on voluntary drivers. Funds would also have to be raised to hire a meeting room in the town. Louth County Hospital stood at the top of a fairly steep hill and a good distance from the bus station. I could see the disappointment on the consultant's face, but on discussion of the difficulties faced, he understood the potential problems involved. However, I remained on the stroke committee until its eventual demise.

After months of rehabilitation, I had regained most of my mobility, and after six months was relieved to get my driving licence, and therefore, my independence back. I continued to enjoy my retirement and my trips over to Derbyshire to stay with Mary. We have enjoyed touring the beautiful countryside and over the years have visited many of the popular tourist sites and stately homes the county has to offer. We also enjoyed regular shopping expeditions to Meadowhall leaving us poorer in pocket but more in the wardrobe! More lately we have taken to utilising the mobility scooters offered free of charge to those with mobility issues. However, I have been known to rear shunt Mary's scooter when her eyes have been suddenly diverted to a shop window displaying 'not-to-be missed' bargains.

Mary and I have been lucky enough to have enjoyed several cruise holidays. On one occasion as we were cruising the Artic Circle, we were issued with tartan rugs to stay the chill as we lounged on deck to see the midnight sun. On that trip we took the opportunity to take a flight by seaplane. Looking down over a glacier I had expected to see glistening white ice, but no, it was a dull cream colour. I commented on this to our pilot who explained that the smoke and ash from the recent eruption of the Icelandic volcano had contaminated the glacier. On another holiday in Cyprus, this time with friends, we had to sweep sand from our balcony. A gale over the African desert had carried the dust over the Mediterranean and deposited it in Larnaca. The natural world can always throw up unexpected surprises.

Cruising the eastern Mediterranean, Mary and I took a trip to the Sphinx and Pyramids of Giza. Scrambling down the inside of one of the pyramids was very claustrophobic and the odour of sweaty humanity was somewhat overpowering! Back in Cairo we were horrified to see electric cables hanging like strings of beads from building to building and any scaffolding was made from bamboo – we were not too sure about their Health and Safety standards!

However, we found our trip to the Church of the Nativity in Bethlehem very moving and invested in some carved wooden animals to supplement the nativity stable at the village church I attended. Each Christmas brought back happy memories of this holiday.

One weekend while staying with Mary I unfortunately had a serious fall involving a visit to the local A&E department at Chesterfield. I was not admitted but was in considerable pain and unable to drive home, necessitating a longer stay. While Mary was at work, her neighbours would call in and make coffee. "Have you thought of moving here, there are two empty bungalows just along the road?" Mary and I thought the matter over and came to the conclusion this could be a good idea. Knowing the likelihood of both properties coming up for sale, I approached the owners directly, and quickly negotiated and agreed a price to buy one just around the corner from Mary.

When I had sufficiently recovered to return home, I started the painful but necessary task of de-cluttering. On answering the front door to a local farmer, "I see an estate agent's sign, are you moving?" I thought I might already have found a buyer for my home, but this was not the case. "Can you look at my leg? I think another varicose vein has burst." Yes, this was clearly evident on the removal of his Wellington boot. I quickly retrieved my first aid box and applied a pressure bandage on his leaking vein. I advised him that he needed to go straight to A&E and telephoned his daughter. She quickly collected him for the trip to Louth Hospital, leaving his tractor parked overnight in my driveway for collection the following morning.

He was my very last patient.

Epilogue

Leaving Theddlethorpe after fifty-six years was a wrench. Dianne, my very good neighbour, helped me downsize and de-clutter in readiness for the move. Her assistance was invaluable, and although she didn't want to lose me as a neighbour, she realised that this move to be nearer Mary was in my best interest. We still keep in touch regularly by telephone.

Mary is the secretary of the Sheffield & District Branch of the Urostomy Association, and I have kept my fingers busy knitting various craft items for sale including snowmen and santa's (each containing a Terry's chocolate orange) and miniature Christmas puddings and sprouts which hold a Ferrero Rocher chocolate. Along with Mary's handmade greetings and Christmas cards, these items are very popular at craft fairs raising much needed funds for the charity. The sale of my home-made whisky marmalade is very popular at the UA branch meetings held in Sheffield, and while Mary is carrying out her secretarial duties, I am the 'sales assistant'.

My new neighbours were very welcoming and I found out later that, on my right, Jackie is a retired nursing sister from Chesterfield Royal Hospital and

Eleanor, on my left, a retired nursing sister from the Royal Hallamshire Hospital in Sheffield. Colloquially our three properties are known as 'NHS Corner' – one can imagine the topics of conversation held over the garden fence!

On bemoaning the fact that I was missing the sound and smell of the sea, Eleanor composed the following poem and it is, with her permission, printed here.

Moving House

I remember the voice of the sea and the wind,
I remember sheets billowing, sails straining to be free,
The washing line dressed overall in towels flapping like
bunting.
I remember the crash of waves booming in the autumn
gale,
reverberating through the headland, careless of
wreckage left behind.
Uncovered treasures, beachcombers.
I remember the gentle breeze, cotton wool clouds,
diving seabirds,
Ebbing tide whispering on sand, caressing rocks,
Leaving pools of wonder for children to explore.
I will name my new home 'Landlocked',
And remember the taste of salt on my lips.